D1544634

the Art of Cooking

MUSCLE SHOALS DISTRICT SERVICE LEAGUE

This cookbook is a collection of favorite recipes,
which are not necessarily original recipes.

*The purpose of the Service League is to foster interest
among its members in the social, economic, educational,
cultural, and civic conditions of the community
and to make effective their volunteer services.*

All proceeds from the sale of *The Art of Cooking*
will be returned to the community through
Muscle Shoals District Service League projects.

Copyright© 1997
Muscle Shoals District Service League
P.O. Box 793
Sheffield, Alabama 35660

Library of Congress Number: 97-076295
ISBN: 0-9620209-1-5

Designed, Edited, and Manufactured by
Favorite Recipes® Press
an imprint of

FRP

P.O. Box 305142
Nashville, Tennessee 37230
1-800-358-0560

Book design: Starletta Polster
Project Manager: Judy Jackson
Art Director: Steve Newman

Manufactured in the United States of America
First Printing: 1997   10,000 copies

*All rights reserved. No part of this book may be reproduced or
transmitted in any form, or by any means, electronic or mechanical,
including photocopying, recording, or by any information storage and
retrieval system, without prior written permission from the
Muscle Shoals District Service League.*

table of contents

The Muscle Shoals District Service League
would like to extend special thanks

To the members and sustaining members of the
League who submitted recipes and
worked so hard to make this book a success

To Favorite Recipes® Press for their
guidance in designing this book

To Dan Jones Ford

To Mitchell Printing Company

FOREWORD

The Art of Cooking confirms that the arts permeate every part of our lives. A beautifully garnished dish stimulates the appetite and is a delight to the eye. The Tennessee Valley Art Association applauds the Muscle Shoals District Service League's newest culinary arts collection.

The MSDSL recognized the importance of the arts in The Shoals when it contributed proceeds from the 1968 Follies to build the Art Center in Tuscumbia. Since the Center's completion in 1972, hundreds of thousands of individuals have benefited from visual and performing arts programs. The League has supported a number of those programs as well as the expansion of facilities.

"Arts in Schools" originated as a collaborative activity between the Service League and TVAA. Through this program over 7,000 fourth grade students in Lauderdale and Colbert counties have received art instruction. There are numerous success stories of children whose social skills and academic performance improved as previously unidentified creative abilities were unleashed. The Ladies of the League serve as good will ambassadors for the TVAA's Arts & Crafts Fair during the annual Helen Keller Festival. Volunteers assist the Fair coordinator and host a recognition breakfast for participating artisans.

The League's reputation for Southern hospitality reaches into communities far beyond the borders of The Shoals and promotes northwest Alabama in a way no paid advertising could begin to convey. Happy little children with painted faces are seen throughout the community during the Festival, thanks to League volunteers who organize and staff the youth activities center.

The League endorsed the Art Association's renovation of the Ritz Theater in Sheffield with a generous donation. Equipment for physically and mentally challenged persons has been funded by the MSDSL. Listening devices for the hearing impaired and water fountains for individuals with physical challenges encourage persons with disabilities to attend visual and performing arts activities by providing for special needs. Equipment for new handicapped facilities at the Art Center has been funded by the League.

The partnership between the Service League and the Tennessee Valley Art Association began in 1968. That continued partnership enables the Art Association to provide creative outlets that promote the mental and emotional health of an entire community of adults and children.

—*Mary Settle Cooney, Director*
Tennessee Valley Art Association

TOMMY MATHIS

Cover artist Tommy Mathis's love of color and nature is eloquently evident in his impressionistic acrylic paintings on canvas. His interpretation of landscapes and florals are filled with light, rhythm, and emotion.

Extensive travel has provided Mathis with ample subjects for his vivid works. Whether large or small, his paintings convey the energy and joy of his love for his favorite settings. He travels with a camera, a sketch pad, and a journal to capture the essence of a location. The paintings born of such trips are usually composites of boats, beaches, houses, rooftops, gardens, street scenes, and sunsets.

"At times I paint from photographs, but more often, I just let go and revisit the place in my imagination!" Mathis remarks with a laugh. "I put shutters, awnings, and umbrellas any place I think they should be."

He has painted series of his native Southeast, the Southwest, the Caribbean, and Europe. "I can enjoy our travels twice: once in reality, and again in my studio," Mathis says. His florals are rich composites of flowers seen and imagined. "Our garden provides many of my floral subjects; the rest are purely fantasy."

Mathis's studio is located next to his home on a bluff, high above the Tennessee River, in rural northern Alabama. He lives with his wife, fashion designer Marigail McCreary Mathis, and their two Himalayan cats, Max and Morgan. Mathis's work is featured in several Southern galleries and in private collections throughout the United States and the Caribbean.

1997-1998 Executive Board of Directors

Debbie Pool	President
Kim Mauldin	President-Elect
Kathy Gamble	Recording Secretary
Lucy Trousdale	Treasurer

1996-1997 Executive Board of Directors

Lynda Darby	President
Debbie Pool	President-Elect
Suzie Alexander	Recording Secretary
Connie McIlwain	Treasurer

Cookbook Officers and Committee

Donna Parkes	Cookbook Chairman
Susan Trousdale	Assistant Cookbook Chairman
Monica Marthaler	Treasurer

Jackie Darby	*The Art of Cooking* Coordinator
Lisa Ruggles	Public Relations
Leslie Ryan	Public Relations

Amy Anderson	Connie Mask
JoAnn Bevis	Kaye Mason
Amy Darby	Pat McAlister
Amy Jon Finch	Loee Miree
Connie Gilley	Kelly Morton
Amy Holcomb	Allison Newton
Dana Lindsey	Cindy Ott
Joni Lumpkin	Julie Shook
Jennifer Marshall	Rhonda Tyree

CONTRIBUTORS

Kay Adkins
Mary Brook Albritton
LeAnn Aldridge
Jan Allen
Amy Anderson
Mary Armstrong
Katherine Bendall
Lynne Bevis
Kathy Brewer
Linda Brocato
Joann Campbell
Marsha Carter
Pam Clepper
Betty Collignon
Lucy Cook
Beth Cox
Amy Darby
Jackie Darby
Lynda Darby
Joanna Edwards
Joyce Elliott
Amy Jon Finch
Cheryl Ford
Kathy Gamble
Nan Gardiner
Julie Gargis
Karen Garner
Connie Gilley
Penny Grissom
Joanna Hardwick
Virginia Hawkins
Connie Hildreth
Amy Holcomb
Stacy Hollaway

Brantley Holt
JoAnn Horton
Jo Beth Hurt
Linda Isbell
Tina Jhin
Faye Johnson
Penny Joiner
Deirdre Kennedy
Joy Little
Joni Lumpkin
Kim Lumpkin
Paula Maloney
Monica Marthaler
Connie Mask
Kaye Mason
Lisa Mathews
Becky Mauldin
Kim Mauldin
Pat McAlister
Connie McIlwain
Caroline McNeilly
Connie Mills
Loee Miree
Simone Mitchell
Susan Mitchell
Holly Morrison
Leigh Ann Morrison
Shawn Nesbitt
Allison Newton
Lydia Nolen
Cindy Ott
Donna Parkes
Sarah Perry
Karran Phillips
Alison Pigg

Debbie Pool
Linda Ray
Susie Ray
Pamela Roberts
Belinda Ross
Lisa Ruggles
Kenda Rusevlyan
Sabrina Scarborough
Melissa Self
Susan Sherrill
Jane Anne Sherrod
Sharon Simpson
Tonya Southall
Teresa Standard
Jeanna Starkey
Keda Stockton
Jackie Stutts
Cindy Tanner
Sherri Tippett
Lisa Trousdale
Lucy Trousdale
Rhonda Tyree
Renée Vandiver
Betty Jo VanSant
Olivia Wages
Lisa Waldrep
Lisa Wallace
Melissa Weatherly
Valerie Wesson
Mary Ann Whitlock
Stephanie Winborn
Martha Woodford
Carolyn Wright
Martha Zuelke

Appetizers & Beverages

Elaine Augustine

ELAINE AUGUSTINE

It is no surprise that Elaine Augustine developed both a love of — and skill at — art. Her grandmother was a professional photographer, and other members of her family have been artists as well. So, Elaine studied art privately and also took art classes while earning a math degree. But a husband, four children, and a family business kept her from pursuing her first love seriously until a few years ago. In just that short time, however, Elaine's works have found their way into private collections across the state, in other regions of the country, in England, and in Puerto Rico. And it's no wonder! Her skill is matched only by her creativity. Equally adept in oils, acrylics, and pastels, Elaine produces colorful landscapes, still lifes, and angels that glow with life. While reminiscent of impressionists, post-impressionists, and even the fauvists, Elaine's style is thoroughly contemporary, though right at home with traditionalists as well. Perhaps it is their simple joy that attracts so many people to her works. In the fast-paced, high-tech, net-surfing world, the simple joys and pleasures are what we need the most.

ARTICHOKE DIP

1 (14-ounce) can artichoke hearts, drained
1 (8-ounce) can sliced water chestnuts, drained
1 cup mayonnaise
1 envelope ranch salad dressing mix

✻ Cut the artichoke hearts into quarters. Combine with the water chestnuts, mayonnaise and salad dressing mix in a bowl and mix well. Chill, covered, for 4 to 5 hours. Serve with wheat crackers.

Yield: 20 servings   Katherine Bendall

HOT ARTICHOKE DIP

1 cup chopped cooked artichokes
1 cup grated Parmesan cheese
1 cup mayonnaise

✻ Combine the artichokes, cheese and mayonnaise in a bowl and mix gently. Spread in a 1½-quart baking dish. Bake at 350 degrees for 20 to 25 minutes or until heated through. Serve with wheat crackers or corn chips.

✻ Note: Frozen artichokes cooked using the package directions work better in this recipe than canned or marinated artichokes.

Yield: 30 servings   Lisa Ruggles

Artichoke Black-Eyed Pea Dip

1 (16-ounce) can black-eyed peas, drained, rinsed
1 (14-ounce) can artichoke hearts, drained, chopped
1 medium white onion, chopped
2 tablespoons grated Parmesan cheese
1/2 cup each sour cream and mayonnaise
1 envelope buttermilk ranch salad dressing mix
4 ounces mozzarella cheese, shredded

❋ Combine the peas, artichoke hearts, onion, Parmesan cheese, sour cream, mayonnaise and salad dressing mix in a bowl and mix well. Spoon into a glass baking dish.

❋ Bake at 350 degrees for 20 minutes. Remove from the oven. Top with the mozzarella cheese. Bake until the mozzarella cheese is melted. Serve warm with corn chips.

Yield: 12 servings   *Kim Mauldin*

Hot Bacon and Swiss Dip

8 ounces cream cheese
1/2 cup mayonnaise
4 ounces Swiss cheese, shredded
2 tablespoons sliced green onions
8 slices bacon, crisp-cooked, crumbled
1/2 cup crushed butter crackers

❋ Microwave the cream cheese on Medium for 30 seconds or until softened. Mix the cream cheese, mayonnaise, Swiss cheese and green onions in a microwave-safe bowl.

❋ Microwave on High for 2 to 4 minutes or until heated through, rotating every 2 minutes. Spoon into a serving dish. Sprinkle with a mixture of the bacon and cracker crumbs. Serve with crackers.

Yield: 10 servings   *Kenda Rusevlyan*

Fabulous Broccoli Dip

2 (10-ounce) packages frozen chopped broccoli
1 large onion, chopped
1/2 cup butter
2 (10-ounce) cans cream of mushroom soup
2 (8-ounce) rolls garlic cheese spread
1 (8-ounce) can mushroom pieces, drained
1 cup slivered almonds
Salt and pepper to taste

Cook the broccoli using the package directions; drain well. Sauté the onion in the butter in a skillet. Add the broccoli, soup and cheese spread and mix well. Simmer until the cheese is melted. Add the mushrooms and almonds and mix well. Season with salt and pepper. Spoon into a chafing dish. Serve hot with large corn chips.

May be prepared several days ahead and stored in the refrigerator. Freezes well. May bake in a 2-quart casserole at 350 degrees for 30 minutes. May top with bread crumbs.

Yield: 50 servings *Kathy Gamble*

California Dip

1 cup shredded Monterey Jack cheese
1 tomato, chopped
4 green onions, thinly sliced
1 (4-ounce) can chopped green chiles
1 (4-ounce) can chopped black olives
3/4 cup Italian salad dressing

Combine the cheese, tomato, green onions, green chiles, olives and salad dressing in a bowl and mix well. Marinate, covered, in the refrigerator for 2 hours. Serve with tortilla chips.

Yield: 25 servings *Caroline McNeilly*

CHEESE AND ONION DIP

1 large egg, beaten
1 cup mayonnaise
⅛ teaspoon pepper
3 cups shredded sharp Cheddar cheese
1 cup chopped onion

❊ Mix the egg, mayonnaise and pepper in a bowl. Stir in the cheese and onion. Spoon into a 1-quart quiche dish or baking dish.

❊ Bake at 325 degrees for 25 minutes. Serve with thin wheat crackers.

Yield: 6 servings   *Brantley Holt*

CHILI CHEESE DIP

1 (15-ounce) can chili without beans
8 ounces French onion dip
8 ounces sharp Cheddar cheese, finely shredded

❊ Spoon the chili into a 7x11-inch casserole. Spread the onion dip over the chili. Top with the cheese.

❊ Bake at 350 degrees until the mixture is bubbly and the cheese is melted. May instead be cooked in a microwave.

Yield: 25 servings   *Donna Parkes*

Incredible Cheese Dip

1 (1-pound) package American cheese, cut into small pieces
1¼ cups water
½ teaspoon each chili powder, paprika and white pepper
1 teaspoon each black pepper and cumin
1 teaspoon minced onion
1 teaspoon minced garlic

❈ Combine the cheese, water, chili powder, paprika, white pepper, black pepper, cumin, onion and garlic in a double boiler and mix well.

❈ Cook over low heat until the cheese is melted, stirring occasionally. Serve with tortilla chips.

Yield: 30 servings   *Pat McAlister*

Feta Cheese and Walnut Dip

1 cup chopped walnuts
¼ to ½ cup fresh parsley
1 cup crumbled feta cheese
½ cup water or milk
1 teaspoon paprika
Cayenne to taste
1 teaspoon olive oil

❈ Combine the walnuts and parsley in a food processor container or blender container. Process in a series of quick spurts until the walnuts are ground. Add the cheese, water, paprika and cayenne. Purée until smooth.

❈ Pour into a small serving bowl. Chill, tightly covered, until serving time. Drizzle with the olive oil. Garnish with small sprigs of fresh oregano or a sprinkling of dried oregano. Serve as a dip for bite-size fresh vegetables or on sesame crackers or toasted pita wedges. May add 1 minced clove of garlic to the cheese mixture.

Yield: 6 servings   *Tonya Southall*

Mexican Cheese Log

16 ounces cream cheese, softened
1 envelope chili seasoning mix
3 tablespoons hot picante sauce
Paprika and cayenne to taste

Mix the cream cheese, seasoning mix and picante sauce in a bowl. Shape into a log. Roll in a mixture of paprika and cayenne.

Yield: 30 servings — *Amy Holcomb*

Paige's Cheese Spread

16 ounces cream cheese, softened
1 bunch green onions, chopped
1 (1-pound) package bacon, crisp-cooked, crumbled
4 ounces Parmesan cheese, grated

Combine the cream cheese, green onions, bacon and Parmesan cheese in a bowl and mix well. Serve with thin wheat crackers or butter crackers.

Yield: 40 servings — *Martha Zuelke*

Easy Fruit Dip

8 ounces cream cheese, softened
1 (7-ounce) jar marshmallow creme

Combine the cream cheese and marshmallow creme in a bowl and mix well. Serve with fruit.

Yield: 50 servings — *Paula Maloney*

OLIVE SPREAD

1 cup sliced salad olives
8 ounces cream cheese, softened
1/2 cup mayonnaise
1/8 teaspoon pepper, or to taste

❈ Drain the olives, reserving 2 tablespoons of the liquid. Combine the olives, reserved liquid, cream cheese, mayonnaise and pepper in a bowl and mix well.

❈ Chill, covered, for 4 to 6 hours. Serve on crackers or cocktail rye bread. Will keep in the refrigerator for up to 2 weeks.

Yield: 40 servings   *Joann Campbell*

GREEN OLIVE TAPENADE

1 1/4 cups pitted green Spanish olives, rinsed, drained
1 tablespoon drained capers
1 large clove of garlic, minced
Juice of 1 lemon
1/4 cup extra-virgin olive oil
1/2 to 1 teaspoon pepper

❈ Combine the olives, capers and garlic in a food processor container. Process until finely chopped. Add the lemon juice and olive oil gradually with the food processor running. Process until mixed.

❈ Spoon into a serving bowl. Season with the pepper. Chill, covered, for up to 24 hours. Serve with assorted crackers, melba toast or toasted baguette slices.

Yield: 15 servings   *Teresa Standard*

PICO DE GALLO

½ cup chopped fresh jalapeños
1 cup very finely chopped sweet onion
2 or 3 tomatoes, finely chopped
2 tablespoons minced garlic
¼ cup chopped fresh cilantro
¼ cup lime juice
2 tablespoons vegetable oil
1 teaspoon sugar
Salt and pepper to taste

❋ Combine the jalapeños, onion, tomatoes, garlic, cilantro, lime juice, oil, sugar, salt and pepper in a nonmetallic bowl and mix well. Let stand at room temperature for 1 hour.

❋ May be used as a dip or served with Mexican food.

Yield: 30 servings

Amy Anderson

QUICK DIP

16 ounces cream cheese, softened
1 (15-ounce) can hot chili without beans
2½ to 3 cups shredded Monterey Jack cheese

❋ Spread the cream cheese in a baking dish. Spoon the chili over the cream cheese. Sprinkle with the Monterey Jack cheese.

❋ Bake at 300 degrees for 10 to 15 minutes or until the Monterey Jack cheese is melted. Serve with chips.

Yield: 50 servings

Jackie Darby

HOMEMADE SALSA

1 (16-ounce) can diced tomatoes
1/4 cup undrained sliced jalapeños
1 tablespoon garlic chips
1 teaspoon garlic salt

❊ Combine the tomatoes, jalapeños, garlic chips and garlic salt in a blender container. Process on high for 1 minute. Serve with taco chips.

Yield: 20 servings   *Karen Garner*

SEAFOOD COCKTAIL SPREAD

8 ounces cream cheese, softened
Leaves of 1/2 head lettuce
1 (8-ounce) jar cocktail sauce
1 (8-ounce) package Louis Kemp crab delights

❊ Place the cream cheese on a bed of lettuce on a serving plate. Top with the cocktail sauce and crab delights. Serve with crackers.

Yield: 25 servings   *Leigh Ann Morrison*

SHRIMP DIP

8 ounces cream cheese, softened
1 (6-ounce) can tiny shrimp, drained
2 tablespoons mayonnaise
1/4 teaspoon each garlic powder and paprika
1 tablespoon chopped parsley
Pepper to taste

❊ Mix all the ingredients in a bowl. Chill, covered, until serving time. Serve with snack crackers.

Yield: 20 servings   *Mary Armstrong*

STEAMED SHRIMP DIP

1½ pounds shrimp, steamed (see Note)
½ tablespoon chopped green onions
2 ribs celery, chopped
8 ounces cream cheese, softened
2 tablespoons each sour cream and mayonnaise
1 teaspoon horseradish
⅛ teaspoon hot sauce, or to taste
½ cup sliced almonds

❀ Peel and devein the shrimp. Chill thoroughly. Chop the shrimp in a food processor. Add the remaining ingredients. Process until mixed. Serve with crackers.

❀ Note: Have the shrimp steamed with mild seasoning at your grocer's.

Yield: 20 servings   *Susan Sherrill*

SALMON MOUSSE

1 envelope unflavored gelatin
2 tablespoons fresh lemon juice
1 small onion, sliced
½ cup boiling water
1 teaspoon salt
1 (16-ounce) can pink salmon, drained, flaked
½ cup mayonnaise
¼ teaspoon paprika
2 tablespoons dillweed
1 cup whipping cream

❀ Process the first 5 ingredients in a blender container for 30 seconds. Add the salmon, mayonnaise, paprika and dillweed. Mix at high speed. Add the whipping cream ⅓ at a time, mixing after each addition. Mix for 30 seconds longer. Pour into an 8- or 9-inch dish or mold. Chill, covered, overnight. Serve with snack crackers.

Yield: 30 servings   *Mary Armstrong*

MONTEREY JACK SALSA

1 (4-ounce) can chopped green chiles
1 (3-ounce) can chopped black olives
4 green onions, chopped
4 ounces Monterey Jack cheese, shredded
1 tomato, chopped
1/2 cup Italian salad dressing
1/4 cup chopped fresh cilantro
Lemon juice or lime juice to taste
Salt and pepper to taste

❋ Combine the green chiles with the remaining ingredients in a bowl and mix well. Serve with tortilla chips.

Yield: 6 servings   *Teresa Standard*

SOMBRERO DIP

1 pound ground beef
1/2 cup chopped onion
2 (8-ounce) cans kidney beans or pinto beans
1 tablespoon each chili powder and salt
1/2 cup chopped jalapeños
1 1/2 cups shredded sharp Cheddar cheese
1/2 cup chopped pimento-stuffed green olives

❋ Brown the ground beef with the onion in a skillet, stirring until the ground beef is crumbly; drain. Mash the undrained kidney beans. Add the mashed beans, chili powder, salt and jalapeños to the ground beef mixture and mix well.

❋ Spread 1 layer of the ground beef mixture in a large baking dish. Sprinkle with some of the cheese and olives. Repeat layers until ingredients are used. Bake at 350 degrees for 15 minutes or until the cheese is melted. Serve with nacho chips.

Yield: 15 servings   *Pam Clepper*

HOT SPINACH DIP

2 (10-ounce) packages frozen chopped spinach
1/2 cup melted butter
2 tablespoons chopped onion
3 tablespoons flour
1/2 cup milk
8 ounces Monterey Jack cheese with jalapeños, shredded
1/2 teaspoon pepper
3/4 teaspoon celery salt
3/4 teaspoon garlic salt
1 tablespoon Worcestershire sauce

❋ Cook the spinach using the package directions; drain well, reserving 1/2 cup of the cooking liquid. Set aside.

❋ Combine the butter, onion and flour in a 1-quart saucepan and mix well. Cook for 1 minute, stirring frequently. Add the reserved liquid and milk gradually, stirring after each addition. Cook until thickened, stirring constantly. Add the cheese, pepper, celery salt, garlic salt and Worcestershire sauce. Cook until the cheese is melted, stirring constantly. Add the spinach and mix well.

❋ Serve hot in a fondue pot or chafing dish with chips, salsa and sour cream. May add chopped jalapeños if desired. The dip may be frozen; thaw and cook until heated through before serving.

Yield: 20 servings   *Sharon Simpson*

TACO DIP

1 pound ground beef
1 envelope taco seasoning mix
1 (8-ounce) jar picante sauce
1 (16-ounce) can refried beans
2 cups shredded Cheddar cheese

❀ Brown the ground beef in a skillet, stirring until crumbly; drain well. Add the taco seasoning mix, picante sauce and beans and mix well. Spoon into a casserole. Sprinkle with the cheese.

❀ Bake at 350 degrees for 15 minutes or until the cheese is melted. Serve with tortilla chips. May add sliced onions and green bell peppers.

Yield: 50 servings   *Holly Morrison*

TOMATO CHEESE SPREAD

8 ounces Cheddar cheese, shredded
1 cup chopped peeled seeded tomatoes
8 ounces cream cheese, softened
1/2 cup margarine, softened
1 small onion, grated
1 teaspoon salt
1/2 teaspoon cayenne
Garlic powder to taste
1 1/2 cups chopped pecans or walnuts

❀ Process the Cheddar cheese, tomatoes, cream cheese, margarine, onion, salt, cayenne and garlic powder in a food processor container until mixed. Shape into a log or ball. Roll in the pecans. Best if prepared 1 day ahead and stored, covered, in the refrigerator. May be frozen for up to 2 months.

❀ Note: To seed a tomato, cut into halves horizontally. Squeeze each half gently; the seeds should fall out.

Yield: 12 servings   *Penny Joiner*

Vegetable Spread

1 envelope unflavored gelatin
¼ cup cold water
¼ cup boiling water
2 cups mayonnaise
1 teaspoon salt
2 to 3 drops of Tabasco sauce
2 medium tomatoes, finely chopped, drained
1 cup drained finely chopped celery
1 small onion, finely chopped, patted dry
1 bell pepper, finely chopped, patted dry
1 cucumber, finely chopped, patted dry

❋ Soften the gelatin in the cold water in a large bowl. Add the boiling water, stirring until the gelatin is dissolved. Let cool.

❋ Fold the mayonnaise into the gelatin. Stir in the salt and Tabasco sauce. Add the tomatoes, celery, onion, bell pepper and cucumber and mix well.

❋ Spoon into a serving bowl or mold. Chill, covered, for 2 to 3 hours. Serve with party bread or crackers.

Yield: 40 servings

Betty Collignon

THE YMCA SPECIAL EDUCATION CAMP, A WEEKLY SUMMER PROGRAM DESIGNED BY SPECIALLY TRAINED EDUCATORS, PROVIDES A PLACE FOR SPECIAL NEEDS CHILDREN TO EXPERIENCE SUMMER CAMP ACTIVITIES SUCH AS ARCHERY, CRAFTS, SWIMMING, HIKING, STORYTELLING, SONGS, SKITS, AND THE RAISING OF THE FLAG. THE YMCA OF THE SHOALS EXTENDS THEIR THANKS "TO ALL OF YOU WHO WORK SO HARD TO KEEP THIS PROGRAM ALIVE AND GROWING. THIS IS WHAT THE MUSCLE SHOALS DISTRICT SERVICE LEAGUE DOES FOR SPECIAL NEEDS PEOPLE OF THE SHOALS."

HEART OF A CHOKE

2 scallions, finely chopped
1 cup seasoned Italian bread crumbs
1/2 cup grated Parmesan cheese
1/2 teaspoon garlic powder
2 tablespoons olive oil
2 (14-ounce) cans artichoke hearts, drained
1 to 2 teaspoons olive oil

❈ Combine the scallions, bread crumbs, cheese, garlic powder and 2 tablespoons olive oil in a bowl and mix well. Roll each artichoke heart in the mixture, packing the stuffing into the top of each artichoke.

❈ Arrange the artichoke hearts in a baking dish. Drizzle with just enough of the remaining 1 to 2 teaspoons olive oil to moisten. Bake at 350 degrees for 20 to 25 minutes or until very brown.

Yield: 8 servings   *Jeanna Starkey*

ARTICHOKE CROSTINI

1 baguette French bread
1 cup each mayonnaise and Parmesan cheese
1 (14-ounce) can artichoke hearts, drained, chopped
1 (4-ounce) can chopped green chiles, drained
2 cloves of garlic, minced

❈ Cut the bread into thirty-six 1/4- to 1/2-inch slices. Place on a foil-lined baking sheet. Bake at 400 degrees for 5 minutes or until lightly browned. Combine the mayonnaise, cheese, artichoke hearts, green chiles and garlic in a bowl and mix well. Spread over the bread slices.

❈ Bake at 400 degrees for 5 minutes or until the cheese is melted. Garnish with chopped green onions, chopped tomatoes and crumbled crisp-cooked bacon. Serve immediately. May use low-fat mayonnaise.

Yield: 36 servings   *Lisa Wallace*

CHEESE STRAWS

1 pound extra-sharp New York cheese, shredded, softened
1 cup margarine, softened, or 1/2 cup each margarine and
    butter, softened
3 cups flour
1/2 to 1 teaspoon red pepper flakes

❋ Beat the cheese and margarine in a mixer bowl until well mixed and very soft. Add the flour 1 cup at a time, beating well after each addition and adding the red pepper flakes with the last addition of flour. If dough is too stiff, knead by hand until well mixed. Spoon the dough into a cookie press fitted with a star tip. Press 2 inches apart onto a nonstick baking sheet.

❋ Bake at 350 degrees for 12 to 15 minutes or until the bottoms are lightly browned. Cool on the baking sheet. Cut into 2- or 3-inch strips. Store in an airtight container or zip-top plastic bag. May be frozen.

Yield: 36 servings   *Betty Jo VanSant*

RICE KRISPIES CHEESE STRAWS

1/2 cup melted butter
1 cup flour
1 cup shredded Cheddar cheese
1 cup Rice Krispies
1/2 teaspoon salt
1/8 teaspoon Tabasco sauce, or to taste
Paprika to taste

❋ Combine the butter, flour, cheese, cereal, salt and Tabasco sauce in a bowl and mix well. Knead on a floured surface until smooth. Shape into quarter-size balls. Place on a baking sheet. Press with a fork to flatten.

❋ Bake at 300 degrees for 15 to 20 minutes or until lightly browned. Sprinkle with paprika.

Yield: 36 servings   *Allison Newton*

CHEESE STRIPS

20 very thin slices bread, crusts trimmed
8 ounces extra-sharp Cheddar cheese, shredded
6 slices bacon, crisp-cooked, crumbled
1 small onion, minced
1 (2-ounce) package slivered almonds
1 cup mayonnaise

❁ Cut the bread into 1-inch strips. Combine the remaining ingredients in a bowl and mix well. Spread over the bread strips. Freeze the bread strips on a baking sheet. Remove to a zip-top plastic bag to store.

❁ Place frozen bread strips on a baking sheet. Bake at 400 degrees for 7 to 8 minutes or until thawed and heated through.

Yield: 60 servings   Mary Ann Whitlock

MARINATED CHEESE

$1/2$ cup each olive oil and white wine vinegar
2 ounces dried pimento, drained
2 to 3 tablespoons chopped green onions
2 to 3 cloves of garlic, minced
1 teaspoon sugar
$3/4$ teaspoon basil
$1/2$ teaspoon each salt and pepper
8 ounces cream cheese, cut into bite-size pieces
8 ounces Cheddar cheese, cut into bite-size pieces

❁ Combine the olive oil, vinegar, pimento, green onions, garlic, sugar, basil, salt and pepper in a jar with a tightfitting lid; cover and shake well. Place the cream cheese pieces and Cheddar cheese pieces in an alternating pattern in a shallow dish or pan. Pour the marinade over the cheese. Chill, covered, for 8 hours. Serve with thin wheat crackers.

Yield: 25 servings   Rhonda Tyree

TUSCAN GRILLED CHICKEN BITES

3/4 cup each chili oil and vegetable oil
1/2 cup soy sauce
1/4 cup white wine Worcestershire sauce
1 tablespoon red pepper flakes
3/4 cup red wine vinegar
3 to 4 cloves of garlic, pressed
1 tablespoon dried Italian seasoning
3 to 4 bay leaves
6 chicken breasts
2 (14-ounce) cans artichoke hearts, drained, cut into quarters
1 cup sun-dried tomatoes, rehydrated
1 bunch green onions, chopped
Pepper Vinegar Dressing

❀ Combine the chili oil, vegetable oil, soy sauce, Worcestershire sauce, red pepper flakes, vinegar, garlic, Italian seasoning and bay leaves in a bowl and mix well. Pour over the chicken in a shallow dish or pan. Marinate, covered, in the refrigerator for 6 hours to overnight.

❀ Remove the chicken from the marinade, discarding the marinade. Grill the chicken until cooked through. Let cool and cut into bite-size pieces. Combine the chicken, artichoke hearts, sun-dried tomatoes, green onions and Pepper Vinegar Dressing in a bowl and toss lightly.

PEPPER VINEGAR DRESSING

1/4 cup pepper vinegar
1/2 cup vegetable oil
Creole seasoning to taste
Nature's Seasoning to taste
Salt, lemon pepper and black pepper to taste

❀ Combine the vinegar, oil, Creole seasoning, Nature's Seasoning, salt, lemon pepper and black pepper in a jar with a tightfitting lid; cover and shake well.

Yield: 20 servings   *Susan Mitchell*

FIG AND APRICOT TORTE

12 ounces dried apricots, cut into strips
1/4 cup banana liqueur
1 1/2 pounds cream cheese, softened
1/2 cup coffee liqueur or Kahlúa
1/4 cup confectioners' sugar
3 cups lightly toasted pine nuts
1 (18-ounce) jar fig jam

※ Combine the apricots and banana liqueur in a microwave-safe bowl. Microwave on High until tender. Set aside to cool.

※ Beat the cream cheese in a mixer bowl until smooth. Add the coffee liqueur and confectioners' sugar and beat until smooth.

※ Sprinkle a heavy layer of pine nuts in a 6-cup mold sprayed with non-stick cooking spray and lined with plastic wrap. Layer the undrained apricots, jam, cream cheese mixture and remaining pine nuts 1/2 at a time in the mold. Chill overnight. Unmold onto a serving platter.

Yield: 30 servings *Susan Mitchell*

HAM ROLL-UPS

8 ounces cream cheese, softened
1 cup finely chopped pecans or walnuts
1 clove of garlic, chopped, mashed
1/4 cup (about) mayonnaise
12 paper-thin slices boiled ham

※ Combine the cream cheese, pecans and garlic in a bowl and mix well. Stir in enough mayonnaise to make of spreading consistency. Spread over each ham slice. Roll up as for jelly rolls. Chill thoroughly. Cut into slices. May serve on round crackers.

Yield: 24 servings *Renée Vandiver*

STUFFED MUSHROOMS

1 pound large mushrooms
4 ounces cream cheese, softened
3/4 cup grated Parmesan cheese
1 tablespoon chopped parsley
2 teaspoons each chopped rosemary and thyme
1/2 teaspoon Worcestershire sauce
Nutmeg, salt and pepper to taste

❊ Rinse the mushrooms and pat dry. Remove the stems and reserve for another use. Combine the remaining ingredients in a bowl and mix well. Spoon into the mushroom caps.

❊ Place the mushroom caps on an ungreased 9x13-inch baking sheet or a baking sheet sprayed with nonstick cooking spray. Bake at 350 degrees for 20 minutes.

Yield: 6 servings   *Jane Anne Sherrod*

EASY SHRIMP-STUFFED MUSHROOMS

10 large mushrooms
2 uncooked stuffed crabs
10 shrimp, peeled, deveined, chopped
2 cups melted margarine
10 ounces mozzarella cheese, shredded

❊ Rinse the mushrooms and pat dry. Remove and chop the stems. Remove the stuffing from the crabs, discarding the crab shells. Combine the crab stuffing, shrimp and mushroom stems in a bowl and mix well. Spoon into the mushroom caps. Place the mushroom caps in a casserole. Pour the margarine into the casserole.

❊ Bake at 350 degrees for 20 minutes. Remove from the oven and sprinkle with the cheese. Bake until the cheese is melted.

Yield: 5 servings   *Keda Stockton*

TOASTED PECANS

1/2 cup butter
1 quart pecans, shelled
Salt to taste

❈ Melt the butter in a heavy skillet. Add the pecans. Cook until heated through, stirring until well coated with butter. Spread the pecans on a large baking sheet.

❈ Bake at 325 degrees for 10 to 15 minutes or until toasted. Drain on paper towels placed over newspaper. Salt the pecans while hot; turn and salt again.

Yield: 15 servings   *Alison Pigg*

COLD PIZZA

16 ounces cream cheese, softened
1 (8-ounce) jar cocktail sauce
1 (4-ounce) can small shrimp
Sliced fresh mushrooms, green bell peppers, onions and
*   black olives*
Shredded mozzarella cheese
Grated Parmesan cheese
Paprika to taste

❈ Spread the cream cheese over a pizza pan or plate of similar size. Spoon the cocktail sauce over the cream cheese. Layer the shrimp, mushrooms, green peppers, onions, olives, mozzarella cheese and Parmesan cheese over the "crust." Sprinkle with paprika. Serve with crackers.

Yield: 12 servings   *Marsha Carter*

QUESADILLAS

¹/₂ cup unsalted butter, softened
8 (7-inch) flour tortillas
4 cups shredded Monterey Jack cheese
8 green onions, minced
¹/₂ cup chopped pimentos
4 pickled jalapeños, minced
1 teaspoon ground cumin

❋ Spread the butter over 1 side of the tortillas. Place buttered side up on a baking sheet. Bake at 400 degrees for 3 minutes or until lightly browned. The tortillas may be prepared and baked up to 2 hours ahead.

❋ Combine the cheese, green onions, pimentos, jalapeños and cumin in a bowl and mix well. Sprinkle over the tortillas. Bake for 5 to 8 minutes or until the cheese is bubbly. Cut into wedges on a cutting board.

❋ May add 2 tablespoons minced fresh cilantro leaves to the cheese mixture. Garnish with sliced black olives, sour cream or avocado slices.

Yield: 8 servings   *Debbie Pool*

APPLES HAVE ALWAYS BEEN GOOD FOR CHILDREN, BUT THE "LADIES IN THE RED STOCKINGS," THROUGH THEIR ANNUAL APPLE ANNIE DAY FUND-RAISER, HAVE PROVIDED A NEW WAY FOR APPLES TO BENEFIT CHILDREN. THE LEAGUE'S DONATION TO WEST WAY CHILD DEVELOPMENT CENTER, INC., IN FLORENCE PROVIDES A CHILD CARE "SCHOLARSHIP" FOR DEPENDABLE, AFFORDABLE, WORRY-FREE CARE FOR AN INFANT OR CHILD UNDER AGE SIX IN AN ENVIRONMENT OFFERERING FUN AND EDUCATIONAL OPPORTUNITIES. THIS PROGRAM ENABLES PARENTS TO WORK OR ATTEND SCHOOL AND KEEP MORE OF THEIR INCOME, SINCE THEY PAY BASED ON FINANCIAL ABILITY. EXECUTIVE DIRECTOR SUSAN WAY ZUBER SAYS, "THE APPLES TRULY ARE A BLESSING FOR WEST WAY'S CHILDREN."

Sausage and Cheese Muffins

1 pound hot sausage
1 (10-ounce) can Cheddar cheese soup
½ soup can water
3 cups baking mix

※ Brown the sausage in a skillet, stirring until crumbly; drain well. Add a mixture of the soup and water. Add the baking mix and mix well; the batter will be lumpy.

※ Spoon into greased miniature muffin cups. Bake at 400 degrees for 10 to 15 minutes or until golden brown.

Yield: 48 servings   Kaye Mason

Easy Hot Sausage with Sorghum

2 pounds Polish sausage, cut into bite-size pieces
2 cups sorghum molasses
Coarsely ground pepper

※ Place the sausage in a 9x13-inch glass baking dish. Pour the molasses over the sausage. Sprinkle generously with pepper. Bake at 250 degrees for 2 hours.

※ Spear with wooden picks to serve. Serve with sweet hot mustard.

Yield: 12 servings   Valerie Wesson

SAUSAGE MUSHROOM PÂTÉ

24 ounces fresh mushrooms, chopped
1 onion, chopped
2 tablespoons chopped fresh parsley
1 tablespoon thyme
2 tablespoons Worcestershire sauce
1/2 cup butter
8 ounces cream cheese, softened
1 pound hot sausage
1/4 cup bread crumbs
1 1/2 eggs, beaten
1 (8-count) can crescent roll dough
1 egg, beaten
1 tablespoon milk

❈ Combine the mushrooms, onion, parsley, thyme, Worcestershire sauce and butter in a skillet. Sauté until the mushrooms are tender; drain well. Add the cream cheese and mix well.

❈ Combine the mushroom mixture, sausage, bread crumbs and 1 1/2 eggs in a bowl and mix well. Spoon into 1 or 2 greased loaf pans.

❈ Bake at 350 degrees for 45 to 60 minutes or until the sausage is cooked through. Drain on layers of paper towels. Cool to room temperature.

❈ Roll the crescent roll dough into a rectangle large enough to enclose the pâté loaf, pressing to seal the perforations. Wrap the dough around the pâté. Brush with a mixture of 1 egg and milk. Bake at 350 degrees for 20 to 30 minutes or until golden brown.

Yield: 12 servings   *Susan Mitchell*

PICKLED SHRIMP

6 cups water
¼ cup crab boil
2½ pounds medium to large shrimp, peeled, deveined
¾ cup distilled vinegar
5 teaspoons celery seeds
2 teaspoons salt
1 teaspoon pepper
1 cup olive oil
1 large red onion, cut into thin rings
3 bay leaves

❈ Combine the water and crab boil in a large saucepan. Boil for 5 minutes. Add the shrimp and remove from the heat. Let stand, covered, for 10 minutes; drain well.

❈ Combine the vinegar, celery seeds, salt and pepper in a food processor container. Add the olive oil in a steady stream with the food processor running. Process for 2 minutes longer.

❈ Layer the shrimp and onion ½ at a time in a shallow bowl. Top with the bay leaves. Pour the vinegar mixture over the layers. Chill, covered, for 24 hours. Remove and discard the bay leaves. Serve cold with crackers.

Yield: 10 servings   *Pat McAlister*

THE BABY LAYETTE PROGRAM OF THE AMERICAN RED CROSS OF NORTHWEST ALABAMA WAS CREATED TO PROVIDE BABY CLOTHES TO AID DISASTER VICTIMS. THE SERVICE LEAGUE BEGINS THE PROCESS BY PURCHASING SUPPLIES OF RIBBON AND FLANNEL FABRIC; VOLUNTEERS THEN CUT AND SEW A BLANKET, GOWN, AND SACK FOR EACH LAYETTE. THE LAYETTES ARE DISTRIBUTED TO SAFEPLACE, RED CROSS DISASTER VICTIMS, OR OTHER CHARITIES IN NEED.

SHRIMP PIZZA

1 (8-count) can crescent roll dough
8 ounces cream cheese, softened
¼ cup salsa
1 rib celery, finely chopped
1 green onion, chopped
½ tomato, chopped
1 (4-ounce) can medium shrimp, rinsed, drained
¼ to ⅓ cup sliced pitted black olives

❈ Separate the dough into 8 triangles. Press over the bottom of a 12-inch pizza pan, sealing the perforations. Bake at 375 degrees for 10 minutes or until golden brown. Let cool.

❈ Mix the cream cheese and salsa in a bowl. Spread over the cooled crust. Top with the celery, onion, tomato, shrimp and olives. Slice into wedges.

Yield: 20 servings   Allison Newton

TACO ROLL-UPS

16 ounces Cheddar cheese, finely shredded
1 (16-ounce) can chunky salsa, strained
1 tablespoon sour cream
16 ounces cream cheese, softened
1 envelope taco seasoning mix
1 (4-ounce) can chopped olives
1 (10-count) package large flour tortillas

❈ Combine the Cheddar cheese, salsa, sour cream, cream cheese, taco seasoning mix and olives in a bowl and mix well. Spread over the tortillas. Roll up and secure with wooden picks. Chill, covered, for 30 minutes. Cut into slices to serve.

Yield: 30 servings   Joanna Edwards

Tortilla Pinwheels

16 ounces cream cheese, softened
1 envelope ranch salad dressing mix
2 green onions, minced
4 (12-inch) flour tortillas
1 (4-ounce) jar chopped pimentos
1 (4-ounce) can chopped green chiles
1 (2-ounce) can sliced black olives

❋ Combine the cream cheese, salad dressing mix and green onions in a bowl and mix well. Spread over the tortillas.

❋ Drain the pimentos, green chiles and olives and blot dry on paper towels. Sprinkle over the cream cheese. Roll up the tortillas tightly.

❋ Chill, covered, for 2 hours or longer. Cut the tortilla rolls into 1-inch pieces, discarding the ends. Serve with the spirals facing up.

Yield: 36 servings   *Lisa Mathews*

SAFEPLACE, INC. OF FLORENCE, ALABAMA, BEGAN PROVIDING SERVICES TO BATTERED ADULTS AND CHILDREN IN 1981. THE MUSCLE SHOALS DISTRICT SERVICE LEAGUE HELPED FUND A SHELTER FOR FAMILY VICTIMS TO LIVE IN SAFETY. IN ADDITION, THROUGHOUT THE YEARS SERVICE LEAGUE MEMBERS HAVE VOLUNTEERED THEIR TIME AND TALENTS IN ANSWERING THE CRISIS LINE, TEACHING CHILD ABUSE PREVENTION PROGRAMS IN SCHOOLS, PROVIDING CHILD CARE, PREPARING LITERATURE FOR OUTREACH AND COMMUNITY EDUCATION PROGRAMS, AND SERVING ON THE BOARD OF DIRECTORS. ARNEDA HEATH, SAFEPLACE'S EXECUTIVE DIRECTOR, SAYS, "THIS YEAR SAFEPLACE WAS ABLE TO MOVE INTO A LARGER, HANDICAPPED-ACCESSIBLE FACILITY WITH THREE TIMES MORE ROOM. A GENEROUS COMMUNITY MADE THIS POSSIBLE, INCLUDING THE SERVICE LEAGUE, WHO CONTRIBUTED SUPPLIES AND FURNISHINGS FOR THE CHILDREN'S THERAPEUTIC PLAYROOM."

Tapenade with Crostini

1 cup pitted kalamata olives
2 tablespoons drained rinsed capers
1½ tablespoons dark rum
½ tablespoon virgin olive oil
½ tablespoon chopped fresh thyme
1 anchovy fillet, rinsed
1 clove of garlic
1 teaspoon fresh lemon juice
½ cup fresh bread crumbs
Freshly ground pepper to taste
1 loaf Italian bread, cut into ¼-inch slices

❋ Combine the olives, capers, rum, olive oil, thyme, anchovy, garlic and lemon juice in a food processor container. Pulse until chopped.

❋ Add the bread crumbs. Pulse until mixed. Season with pepper. May be stored for 1 week in a covered container in the refrigerator.

❋ Arrange the bread slices on a baking sheet. Bake at 400 degrees for 8 minutes or just until beginning to brown. Cool at room temperature on a wire rack.

❋ Spread the anchovy mixture over the bread slices to serve.

Yield: 36 servings   *Pat McAlister*

COFFEE COOLER

> 6 cups cold double-strength coffee
> 4¹/₂ cups 2% milk
> 16 envelopes artificial sweetener
> 1 cup vanilla Coffeemate creamer

❈ Combine the coffee, milk, sweetener and creamer in a 1-gallon container and mix well.

Yield: 16 servings   *Karran Phillips*

MOCHA BLEND

> ¹/₂ cup instant coffee powder
> ³/₄ cup sugar
> 1 cup powdered nondairy coffee creamer
> 2 tablespoons baking cocoa

❈ Combine the coffee powder, sugar, coffee creamer and baking cocoa in a blender container. Process until smooth, scraping the sides once if needed. Store in an airtight container at room temperature for up to several months.

❈ To serve, stir 2 tablespoons Mocha Blend into 1 cup boiling water.

Yield: 19 servings   *Karran Phillips*

COFFEE KAHLÚA PUNCH

4 cups water
1/4 cup instant coffee powder
1/2 cup whipped topping
1/2 cup Kahlúa or amaretto
1/2 teaspoon vanilla extract
1/8 teaspoon salt, or to taste
3 1/2 cups vanilla ice cream

❁ Combine the water and coffee powder in a saucepan. Boil for several minutes. Let cool. Add the whipped topping, Kahlúa, vanilla and salt and mix well. Pour over the ice cream in a punch bowl.

Yield: 16 servings   *Susan Mitchell*

FRUIT PUNCH

1 (24-ounce) bottle white grape juice, chilled
2 (28-ounce) bottles ginger ale, chilled

❁ Combine the grape juice and ginger ale in a punch bowl and mix well. May add 1/2 can pineapple juice.

Yield: 25 servings   *Donna Parkes*

HOT PERCOLATOR PUNCH

2 quarts unsweetened pineapple juice
2 quarts cranberry juice cocktail
1 quart water
2/3 cup packed brown sugar
1 tablespoon whole allspice
1 tablespoon whole cloves
4 cinnamon sticks, broken into pieces
2 large lemons, rinsed, sliced

❈ Pour the pineapple juice, cranberry juice cocktail and water into a 30-cup percolator. Place the brown sugar, allspice, cloves, cinnamon and lemon slices in the percolator basket. Percolate for 30 minutes. Serve hot.

Yield: 30 servings   *Amy Holcomb*

PLEASING PUNCH

2 small packages unsweetened pink lemonade drink mix
1 1/2 cups sugar
1 (46-ounce) can unsweetened pineapple juice

❈ Combine the drink mix, sugar and pineapple juice in a 1-gallon jar with a tightfitting lid. Add enough water to fill the jar. Cover and shake well. Chill until serving time.

Yield: 25 servings   *Stacy Hollaway*

Hot Buttered Rum

1 quart vanilla ice cream, softened
1 (1-pound) package light brown sugar
1 (1-pound) package confectioners' sugar
2 tablespoons nutmeg
2 tablespoons cinnamon
2 cups rum

❋ Combine the ice cream, brown sugar, confectioners' sugar, nutmeg and cinnamon in a freezer-proof container and mix well. Freeze until needed.

❋ To serve, mix 1 shot of rum, 1/4 cup of the ice cream mixture and hot water in a mug. Sprinkle with additional cinnamon and nutmeg. Serve hot garnished with butter.

Yield: 16 servings   *Mary Armstrong*

Summer Tea

1 quart boiling water
6 tea bags
1/2 cup sugar
1/2 cup lemon juice
1/2 cup white grape juice
1 quart cold water

❋ Pour the boiling water over the tea bags in a heat-resistant bowl. Let stand, covered, for 5 minutes. Remove and discard the tea bags. Combine the tea, sugar, lemon juice, grape juice and cold water in a pitcher, stirring until the sugar dissolves. Serve over ice.

Yield: 9 servings   *Debbie Pool*

Breads & Brunch

BRUCE CROWE

BRUCE CROWE

Bruce Crowe, who lives in Russellville, Alabama, is Chairman of the Department of Art at Northwest/Shoals Community College in Phil Campbell, Alabama. His vibrant abstract paintings are created with handmade paper, watercolors, and acrylic paints. His work is well known throughout the South and is included in numerous private and corporate collections. The Montgomery native holds several graduate degrees, including both a Master's degree and a Master of Fine Arts degree from the University of Alabama and a doctorate from Mississippi State University. Bruce has exhibited his works professionally for nearly twenty years and has won numerous awards. His paintings have been selected for such shows as the 43rd National Contemporary American Painting Exhibition, the Scotsdale Watercolor Biennial, Louisiana International Watercolor Show, National Works on Paper, the Central South Exhibitions, and the Watercolor Society of Alabama's National Competitions.

SHARON'S PUMPKIN BREAD

3½ cups flour
1 cup packed brown sugar
2 cups sugar
½ teaspoon baking soda
1½ teaspoons salt
1½ teaspoons allspice
1½ teaspoons nutmeg
2 teaspoons cinnamon
1 (16-ounce) can pumpkin
1 cup vegetable oil
4 eggs
½ cup chopped pecans or walnuts

❊ Sift the flour, brown sugar, sugar, baking soda, salt, allspice, nutmeg and cinnamon together.

❊ Combine the pumpkin, oil and eggs in a large bowl and mix well. Add the flour mixture to the pumpkin mixture gradually, mixing well after each addition. Stir in the pecans.

❊ Spoon into 2 greased and floured 5x9-inch loaf pans. Bake at 300 degrees for 1 hour. May substitute 2 cups fresh pumpkin for the canned pumpkin.

Yield: 24 servings   *Shawn Nesbitt*

JANET BALENTINE, RESIDENT SERVICES DIRECTOR OF THE MITCHELL-HOLLINGSWORTH ANNEX TO ELIZA COFFEE MEMORIAL HOSPITAL, SAYS, "I HOPE THE RELATIONSHIP BETWEEN THE SERVICE LEAGUE AND MITCHELL-HOLLINGSWORTH CONTINUES TO BE AS BENEFICIAL IN THE FUTURE AS IT HAS IN THE PAST. NOT ONLY DO THE SERVICE LEAGUE VOLUNTEERS GIVE THEIR TIME, BUT THEY GIVE A PART OF THEMSELVES TO THE RESIDENTS OF OUR FACILITY."

DIANA'S CRAWFISH BREAD

1/4 cup margarine
2 cups chopped onion
1 cup chopped bell pepper
1 clove of garlic, chopped
1 pound crawfish, peeled
1/3 cup chopped green onions
1 teaspoon salt
1/4 teaspoon pepper
2 tablespoons Tabasco sauce
1 (48-ounce) package frozen bread dough
2 cups shredded mozzarella cheese
1/2 cup melted margarine

❋ Melt 1/4 cup margarine in a large non-iron skillet over medium heat. Add the onion, bell pepper and garlic. Cook until the onion and bell pepper are tender, stirring frequently.

❋ Add the crawfish, green onions, salt, pepper and Tabasco sauce to the onion mixture and mix well. Simmer, covered, for 5 minutes.

❋ Roll 1 loaf of bread dough at a time on a lightly floured surface into a 5x20-inch rectangle. Cut into 5-inch squares.

❋ Spoon 1/4 cup of the crawfish mixture onto each bread square. Top each square with an equal amount of the cheese. Moisten the edges of the bread with water and fold over, pinching to seal.

❋ Shape the bread squares to resemble miniature loaves. Place in a greased baking pan. Brush with some of the melted butter.

❋ Bake at 350 degrees for 25 to 30 minutes or until brown. Brush with the remaining melted butter. Serve warm.

Yield: 12 servings   *Joyce Elliott*

BANANA NUT BREAD

1/2 cup butter, softened
1 cup sugar
2 eggs
3 large or 4 small bananas, mashed
2 cups flour, sifted
1 teaspoon baking soda
1/8 teaspoon salt
1/2 cup chopped pecans

❋ Cream the butter and sugar in a mixer bowl until light and fluffy. Beat in the eggs. Add the bananas and mix well. Add the flour, baking soda, salt and pecans and mix well.

❋ Spoon into a greased and lightly floured loaf pan. Place in a cold oven. Bake at 300 degrees for 1 hour.

Yield: 12 servings   *Joanna Edwards*

BABY BUTTERBALL BISCUITS

1 cup butter or margarine
2 cups self-rising flour
1 cup sour cream

❋ Cut the butter into the flour in a bowl. Stir in the sour cream. Drop by heaping teaspoonfuls into muffin cups.

❋ Bake at 350 degrees for 20 minutes or until firm. The biscuits will not be brown. Serve warm.

Yield: 30 servings   *Kim Lumpkin*

BLUE PETE'S SWEET POTATO BISCUITS

2 to 3 medium sweet potatoes
1/2 cup butter or margarine
1/2 cup sugar
1 teaspoon salt
2 tablespoons milk
3 1/2 to 4 cups flour
4 1/2 teaspoons baking powder
Cinnamon to taste

❀ Boil the sweet potatoes in water to cover in a saucepan until tender; drain well.

❀ Peel and mash the hot sweet potatoes. Place 1 1/2 cups of the sweet potatoes in a large bowl; discard the remaining sweet potatoes or reserve for another use.

❀ Add the butter, sugar, salt and milk to the sweet potatoes in the bowl and mix well.

❀ Sift the flour, baking powder and cinnamon together and add to the sweet potato mixture. Knead until a soft dough forms. Chill, covered, for 30 minutes or longer.

❀ Roll the dough on a lightly floured surface. Cut with a biscuit cutter. Place the biscuits on a greased baking sheet. Bake on the top oven rack at 400 degrees for 15 to 20 minutes or until light golden brown.

Yield: 12 servings   *Cindy Tanner*

CHEESE BISCUITS

8 ounces Cheddar cheese, finely shredded
Salt and pepper to taste
1 cup margarine, softened
2 cups flour
1/2 teaspoon baking powder

❊ Combine the cheese, salt and pepper in a mixer bowl and mix well. Add the margarine. Beat until light and fluffy. Add the flour and baking powder gradually, mixing well after each addition.

❊ Drop by teaspoonfuls onto a nonstick baking sheet. Bake at 350 to 370 degrees for 15 minutes or until lightly browned. Will keep in an airtight container for 1 month.

Yield: 72 servings   *Amy Jon Finch*

EASY CORN BREAD

1 1/2 cups cornmeal
1 (8-ounce) can cream-style corn
1 cup sour cream
1/2 cup vegetable oil
2 eggs

❊ Combine the cornmeal, corn, sour cream, oil and eggs in a bowl and mix well. Spoon into a lightly greased 9- or 10-inch ovenproof skillet. Bake at 400 degrees for 25 to 30 minutes or until golden brown.

Yield: 6 servings   *LeAnn Aldridge*

BEER ROLLS

2 cups baking mix
1/2 cup sugar
2/3 cup beer
1/4 cup butter

❊ Mix the baking mix, sugar and beer in a bowl. Place 1/2 teaspoon butter in each of 24 muffin cups.

❊ Fill the muffin cups 2/3 full with batter. Bake at 350 degrees for 10 minutes or until brown.

Yield: 24 servings   *Mary Armstrong*

MONKEY BREAD

1/2 cup chopped pecans
3 (10-count) cans Hungry Jack biscuits
1 cup sugar
3 tablespoons cinnamon
3/4 cup melted butter or margarine

❊ Sprinkle the pecans into a greased bundt pan or a bundt pan sprayed with nonstick cooking spray. Cut each biscuit into quarters. Mix the sugar and cinnamon in a small bowl. Coat the biscuit pieces in the cinnamon sugar.

❊ Place the biscuit pieces in the bundt pan. Pour the butter over the remaining cinnamon sugar and mix well. Spoon over the biscuit pieces.

❊ Bake at 350 degrees for 30 minutes. Cool in the pan for 3 to 5 minutes. Serve warm.

Yield: 8 servings   *Kim Mauldin*

Cinnamon Rolls

3 cups flour
4 1/2 tablespoons shortening
1 cup milk
1/2 cup butter, softened
1/2 cup each sugar and packed brown sugar
1 tablespoon cinnamon
1 1/4 cups confectioners' sugar
3 tablespoons milk

� Mix the flour, shortening and 1 cup milk in a bowl until a stiff dough forms. Roll into a 12x16-inch rectangle on a floured board. Rub with the butter. Sprinkle with a mixture of the next 3 ingredients. Shape into a log. Cut into 1-inch rolls. Place in a buttered 9x13-inch baking dish. Bake at 375 degrees for 20 to 25 minutes or until browned. Spread with a mixture of the confectioners' sugar and 3 tablespoons milk.

Yield: 12 servings　　　　　　　　　　　　　　　　*Lucy Trousdale*

Raisin Bran Muffins

1 (7-ounce) package Raisin Bran
1 1/2 cups sugar
2 1/2 cups flour
2 1/2 teaspoons baking soda
1/2 teaspoon each salt, cinnamon, nutmeg and cloves
2 eggs, beaten
2 cups buttermilk
1/2 cup vegetable oil
1 teaspoon vanilla extract

✚ Mix the cereal, sugar, flour, baking soda, salt, cinnamon, nutmeg and cloves in a bowl. Mix the eggs, buttermilk, oil and vanilla in a large bowl. Add the flour mixture gradually, mixing well after each addition. Fill greased muffin cups 2/3 full with batter. Bake at 350 degrees for 20 to 25 minutes or until the muffins test done.

Yield: 36 servings　　　　　　　　　　　　　　　　*Keda Stockton*

APPLE RAISIN BRAN MUFFINS

1½ cups oat bran or shredded wheat cereal
1 cup skim milk
¼ cup melted margarine
½ cup honey
1 large cooking apple, peeled, cored, grated
¾ cup raisins
1 egg, beaten
1 teaspoon cinnamon
1¼ cups flour
2 teaspoons baking powder
½ teaspoon baking soda

❁ Soak the cereal in the skim milk in a large bowl for 5 minutes. Stir in the margarine, honey, apple, raisins, egg and cinnamon.

❁ Combine the flour, baking powder and baking soda in a bowl and mix well. Fold the flour mixture into the cereal mixture with a rubber spatula, stirring just enough to moisten; do not overmix.

❁ Spoon into lightly greased muffin cups. Bake at 400 degrees for 20 minutes or until the muffins test done.

Yield: 12 servings   *Lisa Mathews*

JENETTA WADDELL, COORDINATOR OF SPECIAL EDUCATION FOR COLBERT COUNTY SCHOOLS, TELLS US THAT THE LEAGUE "HAS SUPPORTED US WITH FINANCIAL CONTRIBUTIONS FOR MANY YEARS. THIS SUPPORT HAS BEEN USED TO PURCHASE SUPPLEMENTARY INSTRUCTIONAL MATERIALS AND TECHNOLOGY FOR OUR MODERATELY AND SEVERELY DISABLED STUDENTS. THANKS FOR YOUR HELP."

BLUEBERRY MUFFINS

2 cups flour
1/4 teaspoon cinnamon or allspice
1/3 cup shortening
3/4 cup sugar
1 egg
3/4 cup buttermilk
1 teaspoon vanilla extract
1 teaspoon lemon extract
2 tablespoons grated unpeeled lemon
1 cup blueberries
1 1/2 tablespoons sugar
1/2 teaspoon cinnamon
1/2 cup confectioners' sugar
2 tablespoons lemon juice

✻ Mix the flour and 1/4 teaspoon cinnamon together. Cream the shortening and 3/4 cup sugar in a mixer bowl until light and fluffy. Beat in the egg.

✻ Add the flour mixture and buttermilk alternately to the creamed mixture, beating well after each addition. Fold in the vanilla, lemon extract, grated lemon and blueberries.

✻ Fill paper-lined miniature muffin cups 3/4 full with batter. Sprinkle with a mixture of 1 1/2 tablespoons sugar and 1/2 teaspoon cinnamon. Bake at 350 degrees for 20 to 25 minutes or until the muffins test done.

✻ Combine the confectioners' sugar and lemon juice in a bowl and mix until of a glaze consistency. Drizzle over the muffins.

✻ Muffins may be frozen for later use. To reheat, place the muffins in a nonrecycled paper bag in a 350-degree oven. Turn off the oven. Let stand in the closed oven for 15 minutes.

Yield: 36 servings   *Betty Jo VanSant*

BAKED APPLE DOUGHNUTS

1¹/₂ cups self-rising flour
¹/₂ cup sugar
1 egg, beaten
¹/₄ cup milk
¹/₂ teaspoon nutmeg
¹/₃ cup vegetable oil
¹/₂ cup chopped apple
¹/₃ cup margarine, softened
³/₄ cup sugar
1 teaspoon cinnamon

❉ Mix the flour, ¹/₂ cup sugar, egg, milk, nutmeg, oil and apple in a bowl. Spoon into nonstick muffin cups. Bake at 350 degrees for 20 to 25 minutes or until the doughnuts test done. Roll the hot doughnuts in the margarine, then in a mixture of ³/₄ cup sugar and cinnamon.

Yield: 12 servings   *Amy Holcomb*

PANCAKES

1¹/₂ cups flour
¹/₂ teaspoon salt
1 tablespoon baking powder
1¹/₄ cups milk
2 eggs
1 tablespoon corn oil
¹/₄ cup (about) butter

❉ Mix the flour, salt and baking powder in a bowl. Add the milk, eggs and corn oil and stir just until mixed; the batter will be slightly lumpy.

❉ Heat a skillet or griddle hot enough to sizzle a drop of water. Melt the butter in the skillet. Drop the batter by tablespoonfuls into the skillet. Cook for 1 to 2 minutes or until bubbles appear. Turn and cook until browned.

Yield: 4 servings   *Lucy Trousdale*

Sour Cream Coffee Cake

2 cups flour
1 teaspoon baking powder
1/2 teaspoon baking soda
1/2 teaspoon salt
1 cup butter, softened
1 1/4 cups sugar
2 eggs, at room temperature
1 teaspoon vanilla extract
1 cup sour cream
3 tablespoons sugar
1 1/2 teaspoons ground cinnamon
1/2 cup confectioners' sugar

❈ Mix the flour, baking powder, baking soda and salt together. Cream the butter and 1 1/4 cups sugar in a mixer bowl until light and fluffy. Beat in the eggs and vanilla. Add the flour mixture and sour cream alternately to the creamed mixture, beating well after each addition and ending with the flour mixture.

❈ Spread half the batter in a greased and floured 10-inch bundt pan. Sprinkle with a mixture of 3 tablespoons sugar and cinnamon. Top with the remaining batter.

❈ Bake at 350 degrees for 45 minutes or until a wooden pick inserted near the center comes out clean. Cool on a wire rack for 15 minutes. Remove to a serving plate. Sprinkle with the confectioners' sugar.

Yield: 16 servings   *Pat McAlister*

GLAZED SOUR CREAM WALNUT COFFEE CAKE

3 cups flour
2 teaspoons baking powder
1 teaspoon baking soda
1/2 teaspoon salt
2 teaspoons cinnamon
1 1/2 cups sugar
3/4 cup packed light brown sugar
3/4 cup butter, softened
3 eggs
2 cups sour cream
2 teaspoons vanilla extract
1 cup chopped walnuts
Confectioners' Sugar Glaze

❊ Mix the flour, baking powder, baking soda, salt and cinnamon together. Blend the sugar, brown sugar and butter at low speed in a mixer bowl. Add the eggs, sour cream and vanilla and mix well. Add the flour mixture gradually, beating well after each addition. Stir in the walnuts.

❊ Spoon the batter into a greased large loaf pan. Bake at 325 degrees for 1 hour or until the coffee cake tests done. Cool on a wire rack for several minutes. Remove to a serving plate. Drizzle Confectioners' Sugar Glaze over the cooled coffee cake. Do not use margarine in this recipe.

CONFECTIONERS' SUGAR GLAZE

1/2 cup confectioners' sugar
1/4 teaspoon vanilla extract
2 to 3 teaspoons milk

❊ Combine the confectioners' sugar, vanilla and milk in a mixer bowl and beat until smooth.

Yield: 10 servings   *Joyce Elliott*

BREAKFAST ROLL

1³/₄ cups baking mix
¹/₃ cup cold water
3 ounces cream cheese, softened
³/₄ cup shredded Cheddar cheese
8 ounces bacon, crisp-cooked, crumbled
1 egg, lightly beaten
¹/₂ teaspoon poppy seeds

❋ Mix the baking mix and cold water in a bowl until a soft dough forms. Shape into a ball. Knead 10 times on a surface lightly dusted with additional baking mix. Roll into a 12-inch square. Spread cream cheese over the square, leaving a ¹/₄-inch margin around the edges. Sprinkle with the cheese and bacon. Roll up, pinching the edges to seal. Place the roll seam side down on a greased baking sheet. Brush with the egg. Sprinkle with the poppy seeds. Cut slices almost through the roll at 1-inch intervals but leave the roll intact. Bake at 400 degrees for 15 to 20 minutes or until browned. Remove from the oven and cut into slices immediately.

Yield: 4 servings   *Stephanie Winborn*

BREAKFAST PIZZA

1 pound hot or mild bulk pork sausage
1 (8-count) can crescent rolls
2 cups shredded mozzarella cheese
4 eggs, beaten
³/₄ cup milk
Salt and pepper to taste

❋ Brown the sausage in a skillet, stirring until crumbly; drain well. Line the bottom of a greased 9x13-inch baking dish with roll dough, pressing to seal the perforations. Sprinkle with the sausage and cheese. Combine the eggs, milk, salt and pepper in a bowl and mix well. Pour over the sausage and cheese. Bake at 425 degrees for 15 minutes or until set. Let stand for 5 minutes. Serve immediately.

Yield: 8 servings   *Kathy Gamble*

Egg Puffs

1/2 cup margarine
10 eggs
1/2 cup flour
1 teaspoon baking powder
1/2 teaspoon salt
2 (4-ounce) cans green chiles
16 ounces cottage cheese
1 pound Monterey Jack cheese, shredded

❈ Melt the margarine in a 9x13-inch baking pan. Beat the eggs lightly in a large bowl. Add the flour, baking powder and salt and mix well. Add the green chiles, cottage cheese and Monterey Jack cheese and mix well. Spoon into the prepared pan. Bake at 375 degrees for 45 minutes.

Yield: 15 servings   *Joann Campbell*

Cheese and Egg Fondue

6 slices white bread
6 eggs, beaten
2 cups milk
1 tablespoon dry mustard
1 pound Cheddar cheese, shredded

❈ Place the bread slices in a 9x13-inch glass baking dish. Mix the eggs, milk, dry mustard and 3/4 of the cheese in a bowl. Spoon over the bread. Sprinkle with the remaining cheese.

❈ Let stand, covered, in the refrigerator overnight. Let stand at room temperature for 30 minutes before baking. Bake at 350 degrees for 30 to 40 minutes or until the top and sides begin to brown.

Yield: 6 servings   *Allison Newton*

Sausage Mushroom Breakfast Casserole

NOT Good

2¼ cups seasoned croutons
1½ pounds bulk pork sausage
4 eggs, beaten
1 (10-ounce) can cream of mushroom soup
1 (4-ounce) can sliced mushrooms, drained
¾ teaspoon dry mustard
2 cups shredded Cheddar cheese

✵ Spread the croutons in a greased 9x13-inch baking dish. Brown the sausage in a skillet, stirring until crumbly; drain. Sprinkle the sausage over the croutons. Mix the next 4 ingredients in a bowl. Spoon over the sausage. Chill, covered, for 8 hours to overnight. Let stand at room temperature for 30 minutes. Bake, uncovered, at 325 degrees for 30 minutes. Sprinkle with the cheese. Bake until the cheese melts. Garnish with cherry tomatoes.

Yield: 15 servings   Susie Ray

Gourmet Grits

1 quart milk
½ cup butter
1 cup uncooked grits
1 teaspoon salt
½ teaspoon white pepper
1 egg
⅓ cup butter
4 ounces Gruyère or Jarlsberg cheese, shredded
½ cup grated Parmesan cheese

✵ Bring the milk to a boil in a saucepan over medium heat, stirring frequently. Add ½ cup butter and grits. Cook for 5 minutes or until the mixture is the consistency of oatmeal, stirring constantly. Remove from the heat. Add the salt, pepper and egg and mix well. Add ⅓ cup butter and Gruyère cheese and mix well. Spoon into a greased 2-quart casserole. Sprinkle with the Parmesan cheese. Bake at 350 degrees for 1 hour.

Yield: 10 servings   Lisa Wallace

Fresh Tomato Tart

1/2 (15-ounce) package all ready pie pastries
2 cups shredded Mozzarella cheese
2 tablespoons chopped fresh basil
3 medium tomatoes, peeled, cut into 1/2-inch slices
1/2 tablespoon olive oil
1/4 teaspoon salt
1/4 teaspoon pepper
1 tablespoon chopped fresh basil

Fit the pie pastry into a 10-inch tart pan, trimming any excess pastry. Prick the bottom and side of the pastry with a fork. Bake at 400 degrees for 5 minutes.

Sprinkle the cheese evenly into the baked pie shell. Top with 2 tablespoons basil. Arrange the tomato slices evenly in the pie shell. Brush with the olive oil. Sprinkle with salt and pepper.

Place the tart on a baking sheet on the lower oven rack. Bake at 400 degrees for 35 to 40 minutes or until the tomatoes are tender and the crust is browned. Sprinkle with 1 tablespoon basil. Let the tart stand for 5 minutes before serving.

Yield: 10 servings *Belinda Ross*

Alison Isbell, Executive Director of United Cerebral Palsy of Northwest Alabama, Inc., says the League has played a vital role in that organization's operation for years. In addition to donating funds to purchase equipment to help children with special needs, "volunteers through the MSDSL have devoted countless hours to help us achieve our very special task in this community, and we couldn't achieve our goals without them! Thanks for all the help you've given us."

Soups & Salads

Joel G. White

JOEL G. WHITE

Joel G. White knew from a very early age that he had the ability to design and create. He grew up in the nursery landscape business and today has almost thirty years of being involved in gardening and designing landscape plans for residential and commercial clients. A graduate of the University of North Alabama with a B.S. degree in design, Joel completed his Master of Fine Arts degree in design from the University of Memphis. After graduate school he was head of the Design Department at Belhaven College in Jackson, Mississippi, where he taught for six years before moving back to Alabama to open his own art gallery and interior design firm. Joel paints in acrylic. Most are commissioned pieces and can be found in private collections.

Artichoke Soup

1 small onion, chopped
1 tablespoon butter
2 (14-ounce) cans artichoke hearts, drained
2 (6-ounce) jars marinated artichoke hearts
1 (10-ounce) can cream of chicken soup
1 (15-ounce) can chicken broth
Basil to taste
Salt and pepper to taste

✿ Sauté the onion in the butter in a large saucepan. Add all the artichoke hearts, soup, chicken broth and basil and mix well. Season with salt and pepper. Simmer for 30 minutes, stirring occasionally.

Yield: 8 servings   *Amy Holcomb*

Broccoli Soup

1 tablespoon margarine
1 tablespoon chopped onion flakes
4 cups chicken broth
4 ounces egg noodles
1 (10-ounce) package frozen chopped broccoli
2 cups milk
1 (10-ounce) can cream of chicken soup
Salt and pepper to taste
2 cups shredded Cheddar cheese

✿ Melt the margarine in a stockpot. Add the onion flakes and mix well. Add the chicken broth. Bring to a boil. Add the noodles, broccoli, milk, soup, salt and pepper. Cook until the noodles are tender, stirring occasionally. Remove from the heat. Add the cheese, stirring until blended. Serve hot.

Yield: 8 servings   *Jackie Stutts*

Brazilian Black Bean Soup

2 cups dried black beans
6 cups water
1 tablespoon olive oil
3 cups chopped onions
10 medium cloves of garlic, crushed
2 teaspoons cumin
2 to 2¹/₂ teaspoons salt
1 medium carrot, cut into cubes
1 medium bell pepper, chopped
1¹/₂ cups orange juice
Black pepper and cayenne to taste

�֍ Rinse and sort the beans. Soak the beans in 2 cups of the water for 4 hours to overnight; drain and rinse. Combine the beans with 4 cups water in a kettle or Dutch oven. Bring to a boil. Simmer, covered, for 1¹/4 hours or until tender.

✤ Heat the olive oil in a medium skillet. Add the onions, half the garlic, cumin, salt and carrot. Sauté over medium heat until the carrot is tender-crisp.

✤ Add the remaining garlic and bell pepper. Sauté for 10 to 15 minutes or until the vegetables are very tender. Add to the beans and mix well. Stir in the orange juice, black pepper and cayenne.

✤ Purée some or all of the soup in a blender or food processor. Return the purée to the kettle. Simmer over very low heat for 10 to 15 minutes or until heated through.

✤ May add 2 chopped medium tomatoes to the soup when adding the orange juice. Serve decoratively topped with sour cream, cilantro and salsa.

Yield: 8 servings   *Sabrina Scarborough*

Cheese Soup

3 cups water
2 chicken bouillon cubes
4 potatoes, finely chopped
1 medium onion, finely chopped
2 cups finely chopped carrots
3¹/₂ cups warm milk
¹/₃ cup flour
¹/₃ cup butter, softened
1 pound Velveeta cheese, chopped

❀ Mix the first 5 ingredients in a large saucepan. Boil over medium heat for 12 minutes. Remove from the heat. Mix the warm milk, flour and butter in a bowl. Add to the soup. Place the saucepan over low heat. Add the cheese. Cook until the cheese is melted, stirring constantly.

Yield: 10 servings   *Linda Isbell*

Potato Soup

2 cups cubed potatoes
8 slices bacon
1 onion, sliced
2 (10-ounce) cans cream of mushroom soup
2 cups sour cream
¹/₂ to 1 cup (or more) milk
Parsley flakes to taste

❀ Boil the potatoes in water to cover in a saucepan until tender; drain, reserving half the cooking liquid. Fry the bacon in a skillet until crisp; drain well, reserving the drippings. Sauté the onion in the bacon drippings in a skillet. Remove the onion and blot dry. Combine the potatoes, reserved cooking liquid, soup and sour cream in a large saucepan. Simmer until heated through. Crumble the bacon into the soup. Add the sautéed onion. Add enough milk to bring to desired consistency. Simmer, covered, until thickened, stirring occasionally. Sprinkle with parsley flakes.

Yield: 8 servings   *Kaye Mason*

BAKED POTATO SOUP

4 large potatoes, baked
2/3 cup margarine
2/3 cup flour
7 cups milk
4 green onions, sliced
12 slices bacon, crisp-cooked, crumbled
1 1/4 cups shredded Cheddar cheese
1 cup sour cream
3/4 teaspoon salt
1/2 teaspoon pepper

❀ Peel the cooled potatoes and cut into cubes. Melt the margarine in a large stockpot. Stir in the flour. Cook until heated through, stirring until smooth.

❀ Add the milk gradually, mixing well after each addition. Cook until thickened, stirring constantly. Add the potatoes and green onions and mix well. Bring to a boil, stirring constantly; reduce the heat. Simmer for 10 minutes.

❀ Add the bacon, cheese, sour cream, salt and pepper. Cook until the cheese is melted, stirring constantly. Serve immediately.

Yield: 10 servings   *Faye Johnson*

GAZPACHO

4 cups tomato juice
1/2 cup minced onion
1 medium clove of garlic, minced
1 medium bell pepper, minced
1 medium cucumber, peeled, seeded, minced
2 scallions, minced
2 cups freshly chopped tomatoes
Juice of 1/2 lemon
Juice of 1 lime
2 tablespoons wine vinegar
1 teaspoon tarragon
1 teaspoon basil
1/4 to 1/2 teaspoon cumin
1/4 cup freshly minced parsley
2 to 3 tablespoons olive oil
Salt, black pepper and cayenne to taste

❋ Combine the tomato juice, onion, garlic, bell pepper, cucumber, scallions, tomatoes, lemon juice, lime juice, vinegar, tarragon, basil, cumin, parsley and olive oil in a large bowl or container and mix well. Season with salt, black pepper and cayenne. Chill, covered, until very cold. May add 1 teaspoon honey to the tomato mixture. May purée some or all of the soup before serving.

Yield: 6 servings   *Tonya Southall*

TOMATO BASIL SOUP

3 tablespoons butter
1 large onion, sliced
1 large carrot, peeled, grated
4 large tomatoes, peeled, seeded, chopped
1/2 cup lightly packed chopped fresh basil
3/4 teaspoon sugar
1/8 teaspoon pepper
1 3/4 cups chicken broth
Salt to taste

❋ Melt the butter in a 3-quart saucepan over medium heat. Add the onion and carrot. Cook until the onion is translucent, stirring frequently.

❋ Stir in the tomatoes, basil, sugar and pepper. Bring to a boil, stirring constantly; reduce the heat. Simmer, covered, for 10 minutes. Cool slightly.

❋ Purée the soup in a food processor or blender until smooth. Return the soup to the saucepan.

❋ Stir in the chicken broth. Season with salt. Cook until steaming hot, stirring occasionally.

❋ Ladle into bowls. Garnish each serving with thin lemon slices and a basil leaf.

❋ May instead be served cold for luncheon.

Yield: 8 servings   *Debbie Pool*

Easy Ground Beef Vegetable Soup

1 (15-ounce) can cream-style corn
1 (15-ounce) can Veg-all, drained
1 (11-ounce) can vegetable juice cocktail
1 (10-ounce) can chopped tomatoes with green chiles
1 (14-ounce) can stewed tomatoes
1 (15-ounce) can Spanish rice
1 (7-ounce) Polish sausage, chopped
2 pounds lean ground beef or ground turkey

✿ Combine the corn, Veg-all, vegetable juice cocktail, tomatoes with green chiles, stewed tomatoes, Spanish rice and sausage in a medium to large stockpot and mix well. Bring to a simmer.

✿ Brown the ground beef in a skillet, stirring until crumbly; drain well. Add the ground beef to the soup and mix well. Simmer for 30 to 40 minutes or until heated through. May add 8 ounces mushrooms and/or 1 drained 16-ounce can sauerkraut.

Yield: 8 servings   *Brantley Holt*

THE LEIGHTON PUBLIC LIBRARY HAS BENEFITED FROM THE SUPPORT OF THE SERVICE LEAGUE FOR MANY YEARS. LEAGUE MEMBERS HAVE WORKED WITH THE CHILDREN'S STORY HOUR AND HAVE HELPED WITH OTHER LIBRARY PROJECTS. DIRECTOR POLLY KING SAYS, "IN 1997, BECAUSE OF FINANCIAL PROBLEMS IN OUR TOWN WHICH AFFECTED OUR LIBRARY BUDGET, WE WERE AFRAID THAT WE MIGHT HAVE TO REDUCE OUR CHILDREN'S SUMMER READING PROGRAM ACTIVITIES. THE LEAGUE CAME TO OUR RESCUE WITH A GRANT TO SUPPORT THIS VALUABLE PROGRAM. AS A LEAGUE SUSTAINING MEMBER, I AM AWARE OF THE TIME AND WORK THAT IS REQUIRED TO RAISE THE MONEY FOR THE PROJECTS THAT YOU SUPPORT. WE APPRECIATE THAT OUR LIBRARY HAS BENEFITED FROM THESE EFFORTS."

Mexican Taco Soup

1 pound ground chuck or ground turkey
1 large onion, chopped
1 envelope each ranch salad dressing mix and taco seasoning mix
1 (15-ounce) can pinto beans
1 (16-ounce) can ranch-style beans
1 (11-ounce) can whole kernel corn, drained
1 (15-ounce) can chopped tomatoes
1 (10-ounce) can tomatoes with green chiles

✺ Brown the ground chuck with the onion in a skillet, stirring until the ground chuck is crumbly; drain. Mix with the remaining ingredients in a stockpot. Simmer for 1 hour. Serve with shredded cheese and tortilla chips.

Yield: 12 servings   *Rhonda Tyree*

Chili

3 pounds ground beef
2 (15-ounce) cans chili beans
1 onion, chopped
3 tablespoons chili powder
2 (8-ounce) cans tomato sauce
1 tablespoon sugar
1 rib celery, chopped
1/2 bell pepper, chopped
1/2 cup water
Salt and pepper to taste

✺ Brown the ground beef in a skillet, stirring until crumbly; drain well. Cook the chili beans in a saucepan for 15 minutes, stirring occasionally.

✺ Mix the ground beef, chili beans, onion, chili powder, tomato sauce, sugar, celery, bell pepper, water, salt and pepper in a 5-quart saucepan. Cook over medium heat for 30 minutes or until heated through.

Yield: 10 servings   *Sherri Tippett*

BRUNSWICK STEW

1/2 cup flour
1 1/2 teaspoons garlic salt
1/2 teaspoon black pepper
1/2 teaspoon cayenne
1 to 2 pounds boneless skinless chicken breasts,
    cut into 1- to 2-inch pieces
2 tablespoons olive oil
1 large onion, sliced
3 (16-ounce) cans chicken broth
1 (28-ounce) can crushed tomatoes
1 (28-ounce) can chopped tomatoes
1 to 2 tablespoons crumbled fresh thyme
1 (10-ounce) package frozen lima beans
1 (10-ounce) package frozen corn kernels
1/4 cup chopped fresh parsley
2 tablespoons Worcestershire sauce
1/4 cup dry sherry
Tabasco sauce to taste

❀ Combine the flour, garlic salt, black pepper and cayenne in a zip-top plastic bag. Add the chicken pieces, seal the bag and shake until coated.

❀ Heat the olive oil in a heavy large Dutch oven. Add the chicken. Cook until browned, stirring frequently. Stir in the onion. Sauté for 5 minutes.

❀ Add the chicken broth, crushed tomatoes, chopped tomatoes and thyme and mix well. Simmer for 10 minutes.

❀ Add the lima beans, corn, parsley, Worcestershire sauce and sherry and mix well. Bring to a boil; reduce the heat to low. Simmer, covered, for 20 minutes or until heated through. Add Tabasco sauce to taste. Freezes well.

Yield: 10 servings   *Teresa Standard*

CLASSIC LAMB STEW

1¼ pounds lamb leg or shoulder meat
2 cloves of garlic, minced
12 pearl onions
1 (15-ounce) can stewed tomatoes
1 cup cooking wine
2 small potatoes, cut into ¼-inch pieces
2 carrots, cut into ¼-inch pieces
1 rib celery, cut into ¼-inch pieces
2 bay leaves
½ teaspoon dried thyme
¼ teaspoon ground pepper
1 tablespoon cornstarch
¼ cup water

❈ Trim the lamb and cut into ¾-inch pieces. Cook the lamb in water to cover in a 2½-quart saucepan until tender; drain well.

❈ Combine the lamb, garlic and onions in a large saucepan and mix well. Cook, covered, until browned.

❈ Add the tomatoes, wine, potatoes, carrots, celery, bay leaves, thyme and pepper and mix well. Simmer, covered, until the vegetables are tender.

❈ Mix the cornstarch with the water. Stir into the stew. Cook until thickened, stirring frequently. Remove and discard the bay leaves. Stir the stew before serving.

Yield: 4 servings

Pat McAlister

CHERRY CONGEALED SALAD

    1 (6-ounce) package cherry gelatin
    2 cups boiling water
    1 (8-ounce) can crushed pineapple
    1 (21-ounce) can cherry pie filling
    8 ounces cream cheese, softened
    1 cup sour cream
    3/4 cup sugar
    1 cup chopped pecans

❋ Combine the gelatin and boiling water in a bowl, stirring until the gelatin is dissolved. Add the pineapple and cherry pie filling. Spoon the gelatin mixture into a 9x13-inch glass dish. Chill, covered, until set. Combine the cream cheese, sour cream and sugar in a bowl and mix well. Spread over the salad. Sprinkle with the pecans. Chill until serving time.

Yield: 15 servings   *Connie Gilley*

HOLIDAY CRANBERRY MOLD

    3 (3-ounce) packages strawberry gelatin
    3 cups boiling water
    1 3/4 cups sugar
    1 (12-ounce) package fresh cranberries
    2 unpeeled Red Delicious apples
    1 large orange, peeled
    1 cup chopped pecans
    1 (8-ounce) can crushed pineapple

❋ Dissolve the gelatin in the boiling water in a bowl. Add the sugar, stirring until dissolved. Rinse and sort the cranberries. Chop in a food processor. Chop the apples and orange in the food processor. Combine the cranberries, apples and orange in a large bowl and mix well. Add the gelatin mixture and mix well. Add the pecans and undrained pineapple and mix well. Spoon into a lightly oiled large mold. Chill overnight. Unmold onto a lettuce-lined platter. Garnish with orange sections.

Yield: 20 servings   *Olivia Wages*

MANDARIN ORANGE SALAD

3³/4 ounces slivered almonds
2 tablespoons sugar
1 (11-ounce) can mandarin oranges, drained
1 head romaine lettuce, rinsed, drained
¹/2 cup chopped green onions
¹/2 cup chopped celery
Spicy Vinaigrette

❈ Combine the almonds and sugar in a skillet. Cook over medium heat, stirring until the sugar is dissolved and the almonds are coated. Watch carefully as this burns easily. Let cool.

❈ Combine the oranges, lettuce, green onions, celery and almonds in a salad bowl and mix well. Toss with Spicy Vinaigrette just before serving.

SPICY VINAIGRETTE

¹/4 cup wine vinegar
1 tablespoon sugar
¹/2 cup salad oil
2 to 3 drops of Tabasco sauce
Salt and pepper to taste

❈ Combine the vinegar, sugar, salad oil, Tabasco sauce, salt and pepper in a jar with a tightfitting lid; cover and shake well to mix. Chill until very cold.

Yield: 4 servings   *Beth Cox*

Strawberry Pretzel Salad

2 cups crushed pretzels
3/4 cup butter, softened
1/4 cup sugar
16 ounces whipped topping
8 ounces cream cheese, softened
1 cup sugar
1 (6-ounce) package strawberry gelatin
1 3/4 cups boiling water
2 (10-ounce) packages frozen sliced strawberries, thawed, drained

❊ Mix the pretzels, butter and 1/4 cup sugar in a bowl. Press into a 9x13-inch baking pan. Bake at 400 degrees for 8 minutes. Cool. Beat the whipped topping, cream cheese and 1 cup sugar in a mixer bowl until creamy. Spread over the cooled crust. Mix the gelatin, boiling water and strawberries in a bowl. Spoon over the salad. Chill, covered, for several hours.

Yield: 8 servings   *Rhonda Tyree*

Baked Fruit Salad

1 (17-ounce) can apricot halves
1 (20-ounce) can pineapple slices
1 (14-ounce) jar spiced apple rings
1 (29-ounce) can pear halves
3/4 cup sugar
1/4 cup flour
1/2 cup melted butter
1 sleeve butter crackers, crushed

❊ Drain all the fruit, reserving 6 tablespoons of the juice. Arrange all the fruit in a large casserole. Spoon the reserved juice over the fruit. Sprinkle a mixture of the sugar and flour over the fruit. Top with a mixture of the butter and cracker crumbs. Bake at 350 degrees for 1 hour.

Yield: 12 servings   *Cindy Ott*

Frozen Banana and Pineapple Salad

1 cup pineapple juice
1/2 cup lemon juice
1/2 cup each sugar and flour
1/2 teaspoon salt
1 egg, beaten
1/2 cup sugar
1 cup whipping cream, whipped
1 (15-ounce) can pineapple chunks
1 (15-ounce) can Royal Anne cherries
1/3 cup maraschino cherries
4 large bananas, sliced
1 cup chopped pecans

❋ Heat the pineapple juice and lemon juice in a saucepan. Add a mixture of 1/2 cup sugar, flour and salt. Cook until thickened, stirring frequently. Add the egg and 1/2 cup sugar and mix well. Remove from the heat and let cool. Combine the whipped cream, pineapple, Royal Anne cherries, maraschino cherries, bananas and pecans in a bowl and mix gently. Fold into the juice mixture. Spoon into a 9x13-inch freezer-proof glass dish. Freeze until firm.

Yield: 15 servings   Susan Mitchell

Frozen Fruit Salad

1 cup mayonnaise
8 ounces cream cheese, softened
1 cup whipping cream, whipped
1 (16-ounce) can crushed pineapple, drained
1 (4-ounce) jar maraschino cherries, drained, cut into halves
1 (16-ounce) package chopped dates

❋ Beat the mayonnaise and cream cheese in a mixer bowl until light and fluffy. Fold in the whipped cream, pineapple, cherries and dates. Spoon into a salad mold. Freeze until firm.

Yield: 8 servings   Amy Holcomb

Fruit Salad

 1 (16-ounce) can peach pie filling
 1 (10-ounce) package frozen strawberries, thawed
 1 (16-ounce) can pineapple chunks, drained
 2 bananas, sliced
 1 cup chopped pecans

❈ Combine the pie filling, strawberries and pineapple in a bowl and mix well. Spoon into an airtight container. Chill, covered, overnight. Stir in the bananas and pecans just before serving.

Yield: 15 servings   Connie Mask

Fruit Cocktail Salad

 1 to 2 bananas, sliced
 1 to 2 teaspoons lemon juice
 1 (11-ounce) can mandarin oranges
 1 (15-ounce) can fruit cocktail
 1 (15-ounce) can pineapple chunks
 2 tablespoons Tang
 1 (4-ounce) package vanilla instant pudding mix
 1/2 cup sugar

❈ Sprinkle the bananas with the lemon juice. Drain the oranges, fruit cocktail and pineapple, reserving the juice. Mix the bananas, oranges, fruit cocktail and pineapple in a large bowl.

❈ Mix the Tang, pudding mix and reserved fruit juices in a bowl. Spoon over the fruit. Sprinkle with the sugar. Chill, covered, until serving time.

Yield: 8 servings   Lucy Trousdale

ARTICHOKE RICE SALAD

1 (6-ounce) jar marinated artichoke hearts
1 (5-ounce) package chicken Rice-A-Roni, prepared, cooled
5 green onions, chopped
1 green bell pepper, chopped
10 green olives, sliced
1 (2-ounce) package slivered almonds
1/2 cup mayonnaise
1 teaspoon curry powder

�֍ Drain and chop the artichoke hearts, reserving the marinade. Mix the cooled Rice-A-Roni and artichoke hearts in a bowl. Mix in the next 4 ingredients. Mix the mayonnaise, reserved marinade and curry powder in a bowl. Spoon over the salad and mix well. Chill, covered, overnight.

Yield: 6 servings   Connie Gilley

CONGEALED ASPARAGUS SALAD

2 envelopes unflavored gelatin
1/2 cup each cold water and vinegar
1 cup each water and sugar
1/2 teaspoon salt
1 cup chopped celery
1/2 cup chopped pecans
1 (11-ounce) can asparagus spears
Juice of 1 lemon
1 to 2 teaspoons grated onion, or to taste
1 cup (about) mayonnaise
Curry powder to taste

✖ Soften the gelatin in 1/2 cup cold water. Combine the vinegar, 1 cup water, sugar and salt in a saucepan. Bring to a boil. Add the gelatin, stirring until dissolved. Mix in the celery, pecans, asparagus, lemon juice and onion. Spoon into a 9x13-inch glass dish. Chill until set. Top with the mayonnaise, spreading the mayonnaise to the edges. Sprinkle with curry powder.

Yield: 12 servings   Valerie Wesson

Black and White Bean Salad

1 (15-ounce) can black beans, rinsed, drained
1 (15-ounce) can navy beans, rinsed, drained
1 cucumber, chopped
1/2 cup nonfat mayonnaise-type salad dressing
1/2 cup green bell pepper strips
1/2 cup sliced red onion
1/8 teaspoon pepper, or to taste

❋ Combine the black beans, navy beans, cucumber, salad dressing, green pepper, onion and pepper in a bowl and mix well. Chill until serving time. May add 3 tablespoons chopped fresh parsley to the salad.

Yield: 8 servings   *Cheryl Ford*

Fresh Corn and Black-Eyed Pea Salad

1/3 cup balsamic vinegar
1 tablespoon sweet hot mustard
1/4 cup chopped fresh parsley
Salt and pepper to taste
1/2 teaspoon Creole seasoning
1/4 cup olive oil
5 ears fresh corn, cooked
1 (10-ounce) package frozen black-eyed peas, thawed, drained
1 red bell pepper, sliced or chopped
1 Vidalia onion or red onion, chopped
3 ribs celery, chopped

❋ Mix the vinegar, mustard, parsley, salt, pepper and Creole seasoning in a small bowl. Whisk in the olive oil. Remove the corn kernels from the ears with a sharp knife. Combine the corn, peas, red pepper, onion and celery in a salad bowl. Add the dressing and toss well. Chill, covered, for up to 12 hours before serving.

Yield: 6 servings   *Caroline McNeilly*

Colorful Cabbage Salad

2 cups chopped or shredded red cabbage
2 cups chopped or shredded white cabbage
1 red onion, thinly sliced
1 cup grated carrots
1 cup chopped celery
1/2 cup chopped green or red bell pepper
Mustard Vinaigrette

❖ Combine the red cabbage, white cabbage, onion, carrots, celery and green pepper in a large salad bowl and mix well. Pour hot Mustard Vinaigrette over the salad and toss well. Chill, covered, for 24 hours.

Mustard Vinaigrette

1 cup vegetable oil
1 teaspoon salt
1 cup sugar
1 cup white vinegar
1 teaspoon dry mustard
1 teaspoon celery seeds

❖ Combine the oil, salt, sugar, vinegar, mustard and celery seeds in a saucepan and mix well. Heat until the sugar is dissolved, stirring constantly.

Yield: 10 servings *Joy Little*

Corn Salad

2 (12-ounce) cans whole kernel white Shoe Peg corn, drained
1 medium cucumber, chopped
1/2 onion, chopped
1 large tomato, chopped
Sour Cream Dressing

❋ Combine the corn, cucumber, onion and tomato in a large bowl and mix well. Add the Sour Cream Dressing and toss to mix. Chill, covered, overnight.

Sour Cream Dressing

1/2 cup sour cream
1/4 cup mayonnaise
2 tablespoons white vinegar
2 teaspoons salt
1/2 teaspoon dry mustard
1/2 teaspoon celery salt or celery seeds
1/2 teaspoon pepper

❋ Combine the sour cream, mayonnaise, vinegar, salt, mustard, celery salt and pepper in a bowl and mix well.

Yield: 12 servings

Kaye Mason

MOM'S GERMAN POTATO SALAD

5 potatoes
Yolks of 2 hard-cooked eggs
1/4 cup pickle juice
1 tablespoon prepared mustard
1/2 cup mayonnaise
1/2 (5-ounce) can evaporated milk
Salt, pepper and nutmeg to taste
1 to 2 slices bologna, chopped
Chopped parsley to taste

❋ Cook the potatoes in water to cover in a saucepan until tender; drain and let cool. Mix the egg yolks, pickle juice, mustard and mayonnaise in a bowl with a fork. Add the evaporated milk and mix well. Peel the potatoes and slice into a large bowl. Sprinkle with seasonings. Add the mayonnaise mixture and mix slightly with a wooden spoon. Adjust the seasonings. Mix in the bologna. Sprinkle with parsley. Chill, covered, overnight. May add 1 chopped onion to the potato mixture.

Yield: 8 servings   *Monica Marthaler*

DIJON AND DILL POTATO SALAD

1 1/2 pounds potatoes, peeled, cut into cubes
1/4 cup mayonnaise
2 tablespoons Dijon mustard
2 tablespoons chopped fresh dill, or 1 1/2 teaspoons dried dillweed
1 teaspoon salt
1/4 teaspoon pepper

❋ Microwave the potatoes in a microwave-safe bowl, covered with plastic wrap, on High for 8 to 10 minutes or until tender. Cool the potatoes under running water or cover and chill for several minutes. Combine the mayonnaise, Dijon mustard, dill, salt and pepper in a small bowl and mix well. Add to the potatoes, stirring to coat. Chill, covered, until serving time.

Yield: 6 servings   *Jane Anne Sherrod*

Salad with Feta Cheese Dressing

4 cups mixed Bibb red leaf and green leaf salad greens
Feta Cheese Dressing

❋ Combine the salad greens and Feta Cheese Dressing in a large bowl and toss well. Serve immediately. May add sliced black olives.

Feta Cheese Dressing

2 tablespoons finely chopped red or green bell pepper
1 clove of garlic, minced
4 scallions, finely chopped
1 tablespoon chopped fresh parsley
1/4 cup crumbled feta cheese
1/4 cup red wine vinegar
1/4 cup pineapple juice
1/2 teaspoon salt
1/4 teaspoon pepper
1/4 cup olive oil

❋ Combine the red pepper, garlic, scallions, parsley, cheese, vinegar, pineapple juice, salt and pepper in a food processor container or blender container. Add the olive oil in a slow stream with the food processor running. Process until well mixed.

Yield: 4 servings   *Jeanna Starkey*

MIXED GREENS WITH SWEET HOT DRESSING

6 cups torn mixed Bibb lettuce, butter lettuce, radicchio and
  romaine
1/2 cup toasted sliced almonds
1 small purple onion, sliced paper thin
1 (8-ounce) can mandarin oranges, drained
Sweet Hot Dressing

❈ Rinse the salad greens and spin dry. Toss with the almonds, onion and oranges in a large bowl. Pour Sweet Hot Dressing over the salad and toss well. Serve immediately. May omit the oranges and serve with spicy foods.

SWEET HOT DRESSING

1/2 cup vegetable oil
1/2 cup tarragon vinegar
1/2 cup sugar
3 to 5 drops of hot sauce
1/8 teaspoon pepper, or to taste

❈ Combine the oil, vinegar, sugar, hot sauce and pepper in a jar with a tightfitting lid. Cover and shake well to mix.

Yield: 6 servings

Allison Newton

Green Salad with Strawberries and Honey Dressing

4 cups torn mixed salad greens
1 cup crumbled feta cheese
1/2 cup crushed toasted pecans
1 cup sliced strawberries
Honey Dressing

❋ Combine the salad greens, cheese, pecans and strawberries in a large bowl. Add Honey Dressing and toss to coat. Serve immediately.

Honey Dressing

2/3 cup sugar
1 teaspoon dry mustard
1 teaspoon paprika
1 teaspoon celery seeds
1/4 teaspoon salt
1 teaspoon grated onion
1/3 cup cider vinegar
1/3 cup honey
1 cup canola oil

❋ Combine the sugar, mustard, paprika, celery seeds, salt, onion, vinegar and honey in a jar with a tightfitting lid. Drizzle in the canola oil; cover and shake to mix well. Keeps for 1 to 2 weeks in the refrigerator. Bring to room temperature to serve.

Yield: 4 servings   *Connie McIlwain*

Crunchy Romaine Tossed Salad

1 (3-ounce) package ramen noodles
1 cup chopped walnuts or almonds, or 1/2 cup chopped walnuts and 1/2 cup chopped almonds
1/4 cup butter
1 head romaine lettuce, torn
1 bunch broccoli, chopped
4 green onions, chopped
Sweet-and-Sour Sauce

Discard the seasoning packet from the noodles or reserve for another use. Brown the nuts and ramen noodles in the butter in a skillet over low heat, stirring frequently. Drain on paper towels. Store in an airtight container until needed.

Combine the lettuce, broccoli, green onions and noodle mixture in a bowl and mix well. Stir in Sweet-and-Sour Sauce just before serving. May add 1 chopped cooked chicken breast to the lettuce mixture.

Sweet-and-Sour Sauce

1 cup vegetable oil
1 cup sugar
1/2 cup wine vinegar
1 tablespoon soy sauce
Salt and pepper to taste

Combine the oil, sugar, vinegar, soy sauce, salt and pepper in a jar with a tightfitting lid; cover and shake well to mix.

Yield: 8 servings — *Joni Lumpkin*

Layered Spinach Salad

1 (9-ounce) package fresh cheese tortellini
2 cups shredded red cabbage
6 cups torn fresh spinach
2 cups cherry tomatoes
1/2 cup sliced green onions
1 (8-ounce) bottle ranch salad dressing
8 slices bacon, crisp-cooked, crumbled

❈ Cook the pasta using the package directions; drain and rinse with cold water.

❈ Layer the cabbage, spinach, tomatoes and green onions in a large glass bowl. Pour the salad dressing over the top. Sprinkle with the bacon. May add sliced black olives.

Yield: 10 servings   *Karran Phillips*

Spring Salad

4 cups shredded cabbage
1 cup finely chopped green bell pepper
1 cup finely chopped red bell pepper
1 cup finely chopped celery
1/4 cup finely chopped green onions
2/3 cup Italian salad dressing

❈ Combine the cabbage, green pepper, red pepper, celery and green onions in a large bowl. Add the salad dressing and toss well. Marinate, covered, in the refrigerator for 4 hours. Keeps well in the refrigerator for up to 1 week.

Yield: 8 servings   *Karran Phillips*

CHERRY TOMATO SALAD

¹/₄ cup vegetable oil
¹/₄ cup minced parsley
1¹/₂ teaspoons each basil and oregano
¹/₂ teaspoon each salt and sugar
3 tablespoons vinegar
1 quart cherry tomatoes, cut into quarters
4 cups mixed salad greens

❈ Combine the oil, parsley, basil, oregano, salt, sugar and vinegar in a jar with a tightfitting lid; cover and shake well. Pour over the tomatoes in a shallow bowl. Chill, covered, overnight. Serve on a bed of mixed salad greens.

Yield: 4 servings   *Joann Campbell*

ENGLISH PEA CONGEALED SALAD

2 cups canned English peas
1 (3-ounce) package lime gelatin
¹/₂ cup hot water
¹/₄ teaspoon vinegar
¹/₈ teaspoon salt
1 tablespoon chopped onion
1 teaspoon prepared mustard
1 cup mayonnaise
1 cup each grated carrots and chopped celery
1 tablespoon chopped bell pepper

❈ Drain the peas, reserving ¹/₂ cup liquid. Mix the gelatin and hot water in a bowl. Add the reserved liquid and mix well. Add the vinegar, salt, onion, mustard, mayonnaise, carrots, celery and bell pepper and mix well.

❈ Spoon into a 9x9-inch dish. Chill, covered, until set. Cut into squares to serve.

Yield: 9 servings   *Betty Collignon*

Greek Pasta Salad with Balsamic Vinaigrette

12 ounces bow tie pasta
2³/4 cups chopped tomatoes
1 cup chopped cucumber
³/4 cup sliced red onion
¹/3 cup sliced black olives
1 cup chopped green bell pepper
3¹/2 ounces feta cheese, crumbled
¹/2 cup chopped fresh oregano, or 1 tablespoon dried
Balsamic Vinaigrette

✽ Cook the pasta using the package directions; rinse in cold water and drain well. Place in a serving bowl.

✽ Add the tomatoes, cucumber, onion, olives, green pepper, cheese and oregano to the pasta and mix well. Pour Balsamic Vinaigrette over the salad and toss well.

Balsamic Vinaigrette

¹/4 cup olive oil
3 tablespoons lemon juice
2 tablespoons water
2 tablespoons balsamic vinegar
2 teaspoons crushed garlic

✽ Combine the olive oil, lemon juice, water, vinegar and garlic in a jar with a tightfitting lid; cover and shake well.

Yield: 8 servings   *Amy Anderson*

Primavera Salad

    1 pound broccoli
    12 ounces bow tie pasta
    Versatile Vinaigrette
    1 (10-ounce) package fresh spinach
    1 pound smoked turkey breast, cut into thin strips
    1 pint cherry tomatoes, cut into halves
    1/2 cup chopped fresh basil
    1/4 cup each chopped fresh parsley and toasted pine nuts

❀ Remove the leaves from the broccoli; cut off the tough ends of the stalks. Rinse thoroughly and cut into 1-inch pieces. Combine with boiling water to cover in a saucepan. Cook for 1 minute; drain immediately. Plunge the broccoli into ice water to stop the cooking process. Drain and pat dry. Chill until needed.

❀ Cook the pasta using the package directions; drain, rinse with cold water and drain again. Combine with Versatile Vinaigrette in a bowl and toss to coat. Place in a large heavy-duty zip-top plastic bag. Chill for 2 hours to overnight.

❀ Remove the stems from the spinach. Rinse the leaves thoroughly and pat dry. Combine the spinach, pasta, broccoli, turkey, tomatoes, basil, parsley and pine nuts in a large bowl and toss gently.

Versatile Vinaigrette

    2/3 cup vegetable oil
    1/4 cup each white wine vinegar and water
    1 1/2 teaspoons salt
    1 tablespoon freshly ground pepper
    1 clove of garlic, pressed

❀ Combine the oil, vinegar, water, salt, pepper and garlic in a jar with a tightfitting lid; cover and shake well.

Yield: 10 servings   *Melissa Weatherly*

Terrific Tortellini Salad

2 (14-ounce) packages frozen cheese tortellini
1 each green and red bell pepper, chopped
1 cucumber, chopped
1 (14-ounce) can artichoke hearts, rinsed, drained
1 (8-ounce) bottle Caesar salad dressing
1 tomato, cut into wedges

❖ Cook the pasta using the package directions; drain well, rinse with cold water and drain again. Combine the pasta, green pepper, red pepper, cucumber, artichoke hearts and salad dressing in a bowl and mix well. Chill, covered, for 2 hours. To serve, top with the tomato wedges.

Yield: 10 servings *Belinda Ross*

Fruity Chicken Salad

1 (15-ounce) can pineapple tidbits
4 cups chopped cooked chicken
1 (11-ounce) can mandarin oranges, drained
1 (8-ounce) can sliced water chestnuts, drained
1 (2-ounce) package sliced almonds, toasted
1 cup each chopped celery and seedless grape halves
$1\frac{1}{2}$ cups mayonnaise
1 tablespoon soy sauce
1 teaspoon curry powder
1 (3-ounce) can chow mein noodles

❖ Drain the pineapple, reserving 2 tablespoons juice. Combine the pineapple, chicken, oranges, water chestnuts, almonds, celery and grapes in a large bowl and mix well.

❖ Mix the reserved juice, mayonnaise, soy sauce and curry powder in a medium bowl. Add to the chicken mixture and mix well. Chill, covered, until serving time. Stir in the noodles. May serve over lettuce leaves.

Yield: 8 servings *Deirdre Kennedy*

Chicken Salad with Orange Vinaigrette

2¹/₂ cups shredded cooked chicken
Orange Vinaigrette
³/₄ cup mayonnaise
³/₄ cup chopped celery
³/₄ cup chopped grapes
1 (11-ounce) can mandarin oranges, drained
1 (8-ounce) can crushed pineapple, drained
¹/₂ cup slivered almonds

❋ Combine the chicken and Orange Vinaigrette in a bowl and mix well. Marinate, covered, for 20 minutes. Stir in the mayonnaise, celery, grapes, oranges and pineapple. Chill, covered, until serving time.

❋ Spread the almonds on a baking sheet. Bake at 300 degrees for 10 minutes or until toasted. Add the almonds to the salad just before serving. Serve over lettuce with fruit.

Orange Vinaigrette

3 tablespoons vegetable oil
1 tablespoon orange juice
1 tablespoon vinegar
¹/₂ teaspoon salt

❋ Combine the oil, orange juice, vinegar and salt in a jar with a tightfitting lid; cover and shake well.

Yield: 6 servings   *Lynne Bevis*

CURRIED CHICKEN AND ORANGE SALAD

1¼ quarts water
½ teaspoon salt
6 chicken breasts
1 (2-ounce) can black olives, drained, sliced
1 (2-ounce) package slivered almonds, toasted
½ cup chopped purple onion
1 (11-ounce) can mandarin oranges
½ cup plus 2 tablespoons mayonnaise
1 tablespoon lemon juice
1 teaspoon curry powder

❀ Bring the water and salt to a boil in a Dutch oven. Add the chicken. Return to a boil; reduce the heat. Simmer, covered, for 25 to 30 minutes or until the chicken is cooked through. Remove from the heat and let stand to cool; drain well. Cut the chicken into ½-inch pieces, discarding the skin and bones. Combine the chicken, olives, almonds and onion in a large bowl and toss gently.

❀ Drain the oranges, reserving 2 tablespoons juice and 8 orange sections. Combine the reserved juice, mayonnaise, lemon juice and curry powder in a small bowl and mix well. Pour over the chicken mixture and toss gently to coat the chicken. Add the remaining orange sections and toss gently. Chill, covered, for 1 hour or longer.

❀ To serve, spoon into a lettuce-lined bowl or hollowed-out artichokes. Top with the reserved orange sections.

Yield: 8 servings

Julie Gargis

WEST INDIES SALAD

1 medium onion, very finely chopped
1 pound fresh lump crab meat
Salt and pepper to taste
1/2 cup salad oil
6 tablespoons cider vinegar
1/2 cup ice water
8 cups mixed salad greens

❈ Layer half the onion, the crab meat and the remaining onion in a large bowl. Season with salt and pepper. Add the oil, vinegar and water and mix gently. Chill, covered, for 2 to 12 hours. At serving time, toss lightly but do not stir. Serve over the salad greens.

❈ Note: May be served in lettuce cups. To prepare lettuce cups, remove the core from lettuce with a sharp knife. Run cold water into the hole, then gently break the leaves away from the base.

Yield: 8 servings   *Amy Jon Finch*

HONEY POPPY SEED DRESSING

2 1/4 cups mayonnaise or mayonnaise-type salad dressing
1 cup honey
2 teaspoons poppy seeds
1 tablespoon Dijon mustard
Salt and pepper to taste

❈ Combine the mayonnaise, honey, poppy seeds, Dijon mustard, salt and pepper in a jar with a tightfitting lid; cover and shake well to mix.

Yield: 50 servings   *Susan Sherrill*

Meat & Poultry Entrées

PAIGE CATES

PAIGE CATES

Paige Cates is a native of the Shoals area. She graduated with a B.S. in marketing from the University of North Alabama in 1981. Paige is a sustaining member of the Muscle Shoals District Service League. Her appreciation for art began as a young child and has continued throughout her life. Inheriting a love of bright color from her mother, she has only recently begun to explore her creativity through painting.

Meatballs

2 pounds ground beef
3/4 cup cracker crumbs
2 eggs
1/8 teaspoon each garlic, salt, pepper and parsley flakes
1/8 teaspoon Worcestershire sauce
1 (10-ounce) jar grape jelly
1 (12-ounce) bottle chili sauce
1 to 2 tablespoons (about) lemon juice

Mix the first 8 ingredients in a bowl. Shape into meatballs. Place in a 9x13-inch baking pan. Bake at 300 degrees for 30 minutes or until the ground beef is cooked through. Combine the jelly, chili sauce and lemon juice in a saucepan. Bring to a boil. Add the meatballs. Simmer for 5 minutes, stirring occasionally.

Yield: 6 servings *Connie Hildreth*

Barbecued Meatballs

1 pound ground beef
2/3 cup milk
1 small onion, finely chopped
3/4 cup cracker crumbs
1 teaspoon salt
1/2 teaspoon pepper
1/2 cup catsup
2 tablespoons each prepared mustard and brown sugar
1 tablespoon each vinegar and Worcestershire sauce

Mix the ground beef, milk, onion, cracker crumbs, salt and pepper in a bowl. Shape into meatballs. Fry in a nonstick skillet until browned and cooked through; drain. Remove to a microwave-safe bowl. Mix the remaining ingredients in a bowl. Pour over the meatballs. Microwave on High for 5 minutes or until heated through.

Yield: 4 servings *Deirdre Kennedy*

MEAT LOAF

1½ pounds ground beef
1½ cups crumbled cooked corn bread
1 small onion, chopped
Salt and pepper to taste
½ cup tomato sauce
1 egg, beaten
½ cup tomato sauce
2 tablespoons each prepared mustard and vinegar
2 tablespoons brown sugar
⅛ teaspoon Worcestershire sauce

✿ Combine the ground beef, corn bread, onion, salt, pepper, ½ cup tomato sauce and egg in a bowl and mix well. Shape into a loaf in a loaf pan. Mix ½ cup tomato sauce, mustard, vinegar, brown sugar and Worcestershire sauce in a bowl. Spoon over the meat loaf. Bake at 350 degrees for 1 hour, basting every 15 minutes.

Yield: 6 servings   *Jackie Darby*

BEEF STROGANOFF

2 pounds sirloin tip steak, cubed
3 tablespoons butter
Garlic salt and pepper to taste
1 cup tomato juice
1 (10-ounce) can cream of mushroom soup
1 cup sour cream
3 cups hot cooked rice or noodles

✿ Cook the steak in the butter and garlic salt in a saucepan for 20 minutes or until the steak is browned. Add the pepper and tomato juice and mix well. Simmer for 15 minutes. Add the soup and mix well. Simmer for 45 minutes. Stir in the sour cream at serving time. Serve over the rice.

Yield: 4 servings   *Jackie Darby*

Fireside Fillets in Mushroom Sauce

2 cups each sour cream and mayonnaise
1 cup finely chopped chives
1/4 cup red wine
3/4 cup buttermilk
4 to 8 ounces Roquefort cheese, crumbled
1 tablespoon each Worcestershire sauce and fresh lemon juice
1 teaspoon each coarsely ground pepper and white vinegar
1/2 teaspoon each celery seeds and garlic salt
1/2 to 1 cup minced onion
Tabasco sauce to taste
10 (8-ounce) beef fillet steaks
Mushroom Sauce

❋ Mix the sour cream, mayonnaise, chives, wine, buttermilk, cheese, Worcestershire sauce, lemon juice, pepper, vinegar, celery seeds, garlic salt, onion and Tabasco sauce in a large bowl. Pour over the steaks in a 9x13-inch pan. Marinate, covered, in the refrigerator overnight or for up to 72 hours.

❋ Remove the steaks from the marinade, leaving as much marinade on the steaks as possible; discard the remaining marinade. Grill the steaks over hot coals to desired degree of doneness. Remove the steaks to serving plates. Top with Mushroom Sauce.

Mushroom Sauce

1 pound mushrooms, thickly sliced
1/2 cup chopped green onions
3 cloves of garlic, minced
1/4 cup minced fresh parsley
1/2 cup butter

❋ Sauté the mushrooms, green onions, garlic and parsley in the butter in a skillet until the vegetables are tender.

Yield: 10 servings   *Beth Cox*

Rouladen (German Beef Roll-Ups)

1 (2-pound) round steak, 1/4 inch thick
Salt and pepper to taste
1 medium onion, cut into 4 slices
2 slices bacon, cut into halves
1 tablespoon shortening
1 tablespoon flour
1 beef bouillon cube
1/8 teaspoon nutmeg, or to taste

❀ Cut the steak into 4 equal pieces. Sprinkle with salt and pepper. Top each piece with 1 onion slice and 1/2 bacon slice. Roll up and secure with wooden picks, kitchen string or metal skewers.

❀ Heat the shortening in a skillet. Add the steak rolls. Cook until browned on all sides; reduce the heat to low. Cook, covered, for 1 1/2 hours or until the bacon is cooked through and the steak is the desired degree of doneness, adding a small amount of water at a time to keep the steak from sticking.

❀ Remove the steak rolls to a platter. Add enough water for gravy to the drippings in the skillet. Bring to a boil. Thicken with a paste of flour and water. Add the bouillon cube and nutmeg, stirring until the bouillon cube is dissolved. Season with salt and pepper. Serve the gravy with the steak rolls.

Yield: 4 servings   *Monica Marthaler*

Roast Tenderloin of Pork with Mustard Sauce

2½ pounds pork tenderloin
Salt to taste
2 teaspoons pepper
1 teaspoon thyme
2 tablespoons olive oil
1 medium clove of garlic, minced
1 to 2 shallots, minced
½ cup dry red wine
1½ tablespoons Dijon mustard
1 cup beef stock
5 tablespoons whipping cream
¾ cup unsalted butter

Sprinkle the tenderloin with salt, pepper and thyme. Place in a heavy skillet. Sear over high heat for 3 minutes or until browned on all sides. Drain the skillet and set aside.

Remove the tenderloin to a roasting pan. Bake at 450 degrees for 30 minutes or until a meat thermometer registers 160 degrees for medium-rare. Remove the roast to a cutting board and cover lightly with foil.

Heat the olive oil in the skillet. Add the garlic and shallots. Cook over medium heat for several minutes or until lightly browned, stirring frequently. Add the wine. Simmer for 1 minute. Stir in the Dijon mustard and beef stock. Add the whipping cream and stir gently. Bring to a boil; reduce the heat. Simmer for 6 minutes or until the liquid is greatly reduced. Reduce the heat to low. Stir in the butter.

Cut the tenderloin into slices. Top each serving of tenderloin with a spoonful of the sauce.

Yield: 6 servings *Becky Mauldin*

Fletcher's Pork Chops

4 boneless pork chops
Garlic salt and pepper to taste
1 tablespoon each butter and vegetable oil
1 cup sliced mushrooms
1/3 cup dry white wine
1 (10-ounce) can chicken broth
2 tablespoons chopped fresh chives or green onions
1/2 cup whipping cream
4 teaspoons Dijon mustard

Sprinkle the pork chops with garlic salt and pepper. Brown in hot butter and oil in a skillet. Remove and keep warm. Add the mushrooms to the skillet. Sauté briefly. Add the wine, broth and chives. Bring to a boil; reduce to a simmer. Add the pork chops. Simmer for 35 to 40 minutes or until cooked through. Remove the pork chops and keep warm. Add the remaining ingredients to the skillet. Boil until thickened and reduced somewhat, stirring constantly. Spoon over the pork chops. Serve with mashed potatoes.

Yield: 4 servings — *Teresa Standard*

Impossible Bacon Pie

12 slices bacon, crisp-cooked, crumbled
1 cup shredded Cheddar cheese
1/3 cup chopped onion
2 cups milk
4 eggs
1 cup baking mix
1/4 teaspoon salt
1/8 teaspoon pepper

Sprinkle the bacon, cheese and onion in a greased 9-inch pie plate. Process the remaining ingredients in a blender container at high speed for 1 minute. Spoon into the pie plate. Bake at 400 degrees for 35 to 40 minutes or until set. Cool for 5 minutes.

Yield: 4 servings — *Loee Miree*

CREOLE BLACK BEANS

1 1/2 cups chopped onions
1 1/2 cups chopped bell pepper
1 1/2 cups chopped celery
2 tablespoons butter
2 pounds smoked sausage, cut into 1-inch pieces
3 (15-ounce) cans black beans, drained
4 cloves of garlic, chopped
2 teaspoons chopped thyme leaves
1 1/2 teaspoons chopped oregano leaves
1 1/2 teaspoons white pepper
1/4 teaspoon black pepper
1/4 teaspoon cayenne
1 chicken bouillon cube
5 bay leaves
1 (8-ounce) can tomato sauce
1 cup water
6 cups hot cooked rice

Sauté the onions, bell pepper and celery in the butter in a medium saucepan. Spoon into a large slow cooker or stockpot.

Brown the sausage in the same saucepan. Add the sausage, beans, garlic, thyme, oregano, white pepper, black pepper, cayenne, bouillon cube, bay leaves, tomato sauce and water to the celery mixture and mix well.

Simmer over low heat for 4 hours. Remove and discard the bay leaves before serving. Serve over the rice.

Yield: 8 servings   *Rhonda Tyree*

Oven-Baked Jambalaya

2 cups uncooked white rice
1/4 cup chopped green onions
1 (10-ounce) can beef broth
1 (10-ounce) can onion soup
1 (8-ounce) can tomato sauce
1 (8-ounce) can mushrooms
1/2 cup butter
1 pound smoked sausage, sliced
2 pounds shrimp, peeled, deveined
1/2 cup chopped green bell pepper
1/2 cup chopped celery
3 tablespoons parsley
1 teaspoon thyme

❈ Combine the rice, green onions, beef broth, onion soup, tomato sauce, undrained mushrooms, butter, sausage, shrimp, green pepper, celery, parsley and thyme in a large bowl and mix well. Spoon into a greased 9x13-inch glass baking dish. Bake, covered, at 350 degrees for 1½ hours, adding a few tablespoons of water at a time if needed near the end of the baking time.

Yield: 15 servings   *Kathy Gamble*

THE LEAGUE HAS SUPPORTED THE SHOALS AREA TRI-COUNTY ADULT EDUCATION PROGRAM FOR A NUMBER OF YEARS. LEAGUE VOLUNTEERS HAVE PROVIDED ONE-ON-ONE ENCOURAGEMENT AND INSTRUCTION TO ADULTS WHO HAVE EITHER MINIMAL OR NO READING SKILLS. PROGRAM COORDINATOR LIZ ANDERSON SAYS, "NOT ONLY HAS THE LEAGUE HELPED US BY PROVIDING VOLUNTEERS, YOU HAVE PROVIDED FUNDING FOR US TO PURCHASE ADULT-ORIENTED LOW-LEVEL READING MATERIAL, WHICH HELPS FOSTER EXCITEMENT AND ENJOYMENT OF READING. AS A SUSTAINING SERVICE LEAGUE MEMBER, MY HEARTFELT THANKS FOR YOUR GENEROUS SUPPORT OF OUR PROGRAM."

BASIL GRILLED CHICKEN

³/₄ teaspoon coarsely ground pepper
4 skinless chicken breasts
¹/₃ cup melted butter
¹/₄ cup chopped basil
¹/₂ cup butter, softened
2 tablespoons minced fresh basil
1 tablespoon grated Parmesan cheese
¹/₄ teaspoon garlic powder
¹/₈ teaspoon salt
¹/₈ teaspoon pepper

❈ Press ³/₄ teaspoon pepper into the meaty sides of the chicken. Brush with a mixture of ¹/₃ cup butter and ¹/₄ cup basil.

❈ Combine ¹/₂ cup butter, 2 tablespoons basil, cheese, garlic powder, salt and ¹/₈ teaspoon pepper in a small mixer bowl. Beat at low speed until blended and smooth. Remove to a small serving bowl and set aside.

❈ Grill the chicken over medium coals for 8 to 10 minutes per side or until cooked through, basting frequently with the melted butter mixture. Serve the cheese mixture on the side.

Yield: 4 servings   *Teresa Standard*

CHICKEN BREASTS PARISIAN STYLE

1 egg
1 tablespoon water
1/2 teaspoon salt
1/2 teaspoon paprika
4 skinless chicken breasts
3/4 cup finely chopped almonds
2 tablespoons butter or margarine
1 envelope mushroom gravy mix
1/4 cup sour cream

❈ Beat the egg, water, salt and paprika lightly in a shallow pan. Dip the chicken in the egg mixture, then coat with the almonds.

❈ Melt the butter in a shallow casserole. Arrange the chicken skin side down in a single layer in the casserole. Bake at 375 degrees for 50 to 60 minutes or until the chicken is brown and cooked through, turning once.

❈ Prepare the gravy using the package directions. Stir in the sour cream. Heat just to a simmer. Spoon over the chicken to serve. May stir 2 tablespoons sherry into the gravy.

Yield: 4 servings   *Martha Woodford*

MEMBERS OF THE PHYSICAL THERAPY DEPARTMENT AT THE NORTHWEST ALABAMA EASTER SEAL REHABILITATION CENTER SAY THAT "WITHOUT YOUR [MSDSL] FINANCIAL SUPPORT THE PHYSICAL THERAPY DEPARTMENT COULD NOT HAVE THE EQUIPMENT NEEDED TO WORK WITH THESE CHILDREN AND ADULTS. OUR TREADMILL, OUR SPORTS RIDER, OUR RECUMBENT BIKE, AND OUR PEDIATRIC TRICYCLE HAVE BEEN A TREMENDOUS HELP."

Citrus Grilled Chicken

1/2 cup mayonnaise-type salad dressing
1 tablespoon lime juice
1/2 teaspoon garlic powder
1/2 teaspoon ground red pepper
1/2 teaspoon ground cumin
4 boneless skinless chicken breasts

✖ Mix the salad dressing, lime juice, garlic powder, pepper and cumin in a bowl. Spoon over the chicken in a shallow pan. Marinate, covered, in the refrigerator for 30 minutes or longer. Remove the chicken from the marinade, discarding the marinade.

✖ Place the chicken on a grill rack over medium coals or on the rack of a broiler pan 5 to 7 inches from the heat source. Grill or broil for 8 to 10 minutes per side or until the chicken is cooked through, turning once.

Yield: 4 servings   *Joann Campbell*

Lemon Mustard Chicken

6 skinless chicken breasts
1/4 cup margarine
3 tablespoons Dijon mustard
3 tablespoons fresh lemon juice
1 teaspoon tarragon
1/2 teaspoon salt

✖ Place the chicken in a shallow baking pan. Melt the margarine in a small saucepan. Stir in the Dijon mustard, lemon juice, tarragon and salt. Spoon over the chicken.

✖ Bake at 375 degrees for 45 minutes or until the chicken is cooked through. Spoon the pan drippings over the chicken to serve. Serve with cooked rice.

Yield: 6 servings   *Marsha Carter*

Raspberry Chicken

2 whole boneless skinless chicken breasts
2 tablespoons unsalted butter
¼ cup finely chopped onion
¼ cup raspberry vinegar
¼ cup chicken stock or chicken broth
¼ cup whipping cream
1 tablespoon canned crushed tomatoes
16 fresh raspberries

✽ Cut each piece of chicken into halves along the breast bone. Flatten gently with the palm of the hand.

✽ Melt the butter in a large skillet over medium heat. Add the chicken. Cook for 3 minutes per side or until light brown. Remove the chicken and keep warm.

✽ Add the onion to the skillet. Cook over low heat for 15 minutes or until tender, stirring frequently.

✽ Add the vinegar and increase the heat. Cook until the vinegar is syrupy, stirring occasionally. Whisk in the chicken stock, whipping cream and tomatoes. Simmer for 1 minute.

✽ Return the chicken to the skillet. Simmer in the sauce for 5 minutes or until cooked through. Remove the chicken to a serving platter.

✽ Cook the sauce over low heat for 1 to 2 minutes or until heated through. Add the raspberries without stirring. Spoon the sauce over the chicken. Serve immediately.

Yield: 4 servings   *Lisa Wallace*

Chicken in Sour Cream

2 whole chicken breasts
1 (10-ounce) can cream of chicken soup
1 cup sour cream
1 sleeve crackers
1/2 cup melted margarine
4 1/2 cups hot cooked rice

✿ Cook the chicken in water to cover in a saucepan until tender; drain, reserving 10 ounces of the broth. Debone the chicken.

✿ Arrange the chicken in a baking dish. Mix the soup and reserved broth in a bowl. Fold in the sour cream. Spoon over the chicken. Crumble the crackers over the top. Drizzle with the margarine. Bake at 350 degrees for 30 minutes. Serve over the rice.

Yield: 6 servings   *Jackie Darby*

Susie's Chicken and White Sauce

1 cup mayonnaise
1/4 cup vinegar
1/4 cup lemon juice
1 tablespoon salt, or to taste
1 tablespoon pepper, or to taste
6 chicken breasts

✿ Mix the mayonnaise, vinegar, lemon juice, salt and pepper in a bowl. Spoon most of the mixture over the chicken in a baking dish. Bake at 350 degrees for 1 hour or until the chicken is cooked through. Serve with the remaining sauce. The sauce may be prepared using mayonnaise-type salad dressing; the taste will be different but still very good.

Yield: 6 servings   *Susie Ray*

CHICKEN QUESADILLAS

4 boneless skinless chicken breasts
1 envelope taco seasoning mix
2 1/2 cups shredded Monterey Jack cheese
2/3 cup picante sauce
1 medium red bell pepper, chopped
10 (10-inch) flour tortillas
5 teaspoons (about) melted butter

❉ Combine the chicken and taco seasoning mix in a heavy-duty zip-top plastic bag and shake to coat. Chill for 1 hour. Remove the chicken from the plastic bag. Arrange in a single layer in a 10x15-inch baking pan. Broil for 5 minutes 6 inches from the heat source with the oven door ajar. Let the chicken cool before chopping or shredding. Combine the chicken, cheese, picante sauce and red pepper in a bowl and mix well.

❉ Brush 1 side of each tortilla with butter. Place half the tortillas buttered side up on baking sheets. Spoon 1 cup of the chicken mixture onto each tortilla on the baking sheets. Top with the remaining tortillas buttered side up. Bake at 375 degrees for 10 minutes or until the quesadillas are golden brown. Cut into wedges.

Yield: 5 servings   *Susie Ray*

THE ROLLING RIDERS PROGRAM PROVIDES THERAPEUTIC HORSEBACK RIDING AND EDUCATIONAL OPPORTUNITIES TO BENEFIT CHILDREN WITH PHYSICAL, EMOTIONAL, AND BEHAVIORAL PROBLEMS. THE LEAGUE WAS ABLE TO PROVIDE SEED MONEY FOR THIS PROGRAM FOR SPECIALLY OUTFITTED EQUIPMENT FOR THESE SPECIAL RIDERS. EXECUTIVE DIRECTOR NANCY SQUIRES SAYS, "THIS WAS A TREMENDOUS HELP TO ROLLING RIDERS. AGAIN, MANY, MANY THANKS FOR YOUR CONTINUED INTEREST AND SUPPORT."

HOT CHICKEN SALAD PIE

2 cups chopped cooked chicken
1 1/2 cups chopped celery
1 teaspoon each grated onion and salt
1/4 teaspoon MSG
1 teaspoon lemon juice
1/3 cup chopped pecans
1 1/2 cups mayonnaise
1 baked (9-inch) pie shell
1 cup crushed potato chips
1/2 cup shredded Cheddar cheese

❈ Mix the chicken, celery, onion, salt, MSG, lemon juice, pecans and mayonnaise in a bowl. Spoon into the pie shell. Top with the potato chips and cheese. Bake at 350 degrees for 20 to 30 minutes or until heated through.

Yield: 6 servings   Renée Vandiver

ROASTED DUCK BREAST

4 duck breast fillets
1 Granny Smith apple, cut into 8 slices
8 slices bacon
1 1/2 sticks (3/4 cup) butter, sliced
1 bay leaf, crushed
1 tablespoon poultry seasoning
1 teaspoon each parsley flakes and salt
1/8 teaspoon each black pepper, red pepper flakes and cinnamon

❈ Line a baking dish with a large piece of foil. Cut a slit in the side of each fillet to form a pocket. Insert 2 apple slices into each pocket. Wrap the fillets in bacon. Arrange in the baking dish. Top with the butter. Sprinkle with the bay leaf, poultry seasoning, parsley flakes, salt, black pepper, red pepper and cinnamon. Seal the foil tightly. Bake at 350 degrees for 1 1/4 hours. Serve with wild rice and steamed fresh vegetables.

Yield: 4 servings   Allison Newton

COMEBACK SAUCE

1/2 cup mayonnaise
1/4 cup olive oil
3 tablespoons chili sauce
2 tablespoons catsup
1 tablespoon water
2 teaspoons Worcestershire sauce
2 teaspoons prepared mustard
1 teaspoon pepper
1/8 teaspoon paprika, or to taste
1/8 teaspoon hot sauce, or to taste
1 small onion, minced
1 clove of garlic, minced

❀ Combine the mayonnaise, olive oil, chili sauce, catsup, water, Worcestershire sauce, mustard, pepper, paprika, hot sauce, onion and garlic in a bowl and mix well. Serve with chicken fingers.

Yield: 20 servings   *Amy Holcomb*

GREAT WHITE BARBECUE SAUCE

6 tablespoons mayonnaise
1 tablespoon salt
1 tablespoon pepper
1 tablespoon white vinegar
1 teaspoon sugar
Juice of 1/2 lemon

❀ Mix the mayonnaise, salt, pepper, vinegar, sugar and lemon juice in a bowl. Serve over baked or grilled chicken.

Yield: 10 servings   *Karran Phillips*

Seafood & Pasta Entrées

SAMUEL WILLIAM BARNETT

SAMUEL WILLIAM BARNETT

Samuel William Barnett gained his interest and respect for watercolor painting while attending Auburn University's College of Architecture and Fine Arts. While studying for a degree in landscape architecture, the artist utilized this medium to render various designs and illustrations. Inspired by the works of John Singer Sargent, the Wyeth family, and Edward Hopper, Mr. Barnett built his career in landscape architecture while simultaneously working toward developing skills as a watercolor artist. This process eventually led to portraiture, where a combination of watercolor and watercolor drybrush techniques is employed. In concert with these techniques, the basic design principles of form, rhythm, order, color, and texture are employed to achieve solidly conceived paintings. Mr. Barnett maintains his landscape architectural practice to parallel his career as an artist, portraitist, and illustrator, thus reinforcing the basic elements of design.

Coquilles St. Jacques Baumanière (Scallops in Cream Sauce)

1 cup flour
2 eggs
1³/4 cups milk
¹/2 teaspoon salt
1 tablespoon melted butter
1¹/2 pounds scallops
1 tablespoon chopped shallots
¹/4 teaspoon salt
¹/8 teaspoon white pepper, or to taste
¹/2 cup dry vermouth
1 cup whipping cream
1 tablespoon flour
¹/4 cup butter, softened

❀ For the crepes, mix 1 cup flour and eggs in a bowl with a wire whisk. Add the milk, ¹/2 teaspoon salt and 1 tablespoon butter and mix well. Heat a greased crepe pan, omelet pan or other nonstick pan over medium-high heat. Pour ¹/4 to ¹/3 cup of the batter into the hot pan. Cook quickly until golden brown on each side. Set aside and keep warm. Repeat the process with the remaining batter.

❀ For the sauce, rinse the scallops; cut any large scallops into quarters. Combine with the shallots, ¹/4 teaspoon salt, pepper and vermouth in a saucepan. Bring to a boil; reduce the heat to low. Simmer, covered, for exactly 2 minutes. Remove the scallops with a slotted spoon and set aside. Increase the heat to high. Cook until the liquid is reduced by ¹/2. Add the whipping cream. Boil rapidly until the sauce is the consistency of syrup. Reduce the heat. Stir in a mixture of 1 tablespoon flour and ¹/4 cup butter gradually.

❀ Place several scallops and a small amount of the sauce in the center of each crepe. Roll up each crepe. Place seam side down in a baking dish. Cover with the remaining sauce. Bake, covered with foil, at 450 degrees for 5 minutes. May substitute shrimp for the scallops or use a mixture of scallops and shrimp.

Yield: 4 servings   *Lisa Mathews*

SHRIMP CREOLE

1/4 cup margarine
1 large onion, chopped
1 large clove of garlic, minced
1/2 cup chopped green bell pepper
1/2 cup chopped celery
2 tablespoons flour
1 to 2 tablespoons salt
1/2 teaspoon black pepper
1/4 teaspoon red pepper flakes
1 (16-ounce) can tomatoes
1 (8-ounce) can tomato sauce
3 sprigs of fresh parsley, chopped
4 small green onions, chopped
1/2 cup water
1 pound shrimp, peeled, deveined
4 1/2 cups hot cooked rice

❀ Melt the margarine in a large skillet. Add the onion, garlic, green pepper and celery. Sauté until the onion is lightly browned. Blend in the flour.

❀ Add the salt, black pepper, red pepper, tomatoes, tomato sauce, parsley, green onions and water to the onion mixture in the skillet and mix well. Bring to a boil. Simmer, covered, for 30 minutes. Stir in the shrimp. Cook, covered, for 10 minutes. Serve over the rice.

Yield: 6 servings   *Kathy Brewer*

Marinated Shrimp Kabobs

1½ pounds fresh shrimp
1 (8-ounce) can pineapple chunks
2 tablespoons vegetable oil
2 tablespoons soy sauce
¼ teaspoon white pepper
⅛ teaspoon garlic powder
⅛ teaspoon ground ginger
16 to 24 pearl onions
16 to 24 cherry tomatoes
2 green bell peppers, sliced
4 cups hot cooked rice

✽ Peel and devein the shrimp, leaving the tails intact. Mix the undrained pineapple, oil, soy sauce, pepper, garlic powder and ginger in a shallow dish. Add the shrimp, tossing gently to coat. Marinate, covered, in the refrigerator for 1 hour or longer, stirring occasionally.

✽ Cook the onions in water to cover in a saucepan for 4 to 5 minutes or just until tender-crisp. Remove the shrimp from the marinade, reserving the marinade. Thread the shrimp, onions, tomatoes and green pepper alternately onto skewers. Broil or grill 4 to 5 inches from the heat source for 2 to 3 minutes per side or until the shrimp turn pink, basting occasionally with marinade. Serve over the rice.

Yield: 4 servings   Lynda Darby

SKILLET BARBECUED SHRIMP

1 teaspoon cayenne, or to taste
1 teaspoon black pepper, or to taste
1/2 teaspoon crushed red pepper, or to taste
1/2 teaspoon salt
1/2 teaspoon dried thyme leaves
1/2 teaspoon dried rosemary leaves
1/4 teaspoon dried oregano leaves
1/2 teaspoon paprika
1/2 teaspoon barbecue seasoning
1/2 cup butter
1 1/2 teaspoons minced garlic
1 teaspoon Worcestershire sauce
1 1/2 pounds large shrimp, peeled, deveined
1/4 cup butter
1/2 cup seafood stock
1/4 cup beer

❈ Combine the cayenne, black pepper, red pepper, salt, thyme, rosemary, oregano, paprika and barbecue seasoning in a small bowl and mix well.

❈ Combine 1/2 cup butter, garlic, Worcestershire sauce and the pepper mixture in a cast-iron skillet over high heat. Add the shrimp. Cook for 2 minutes, shaking the pan constantly but without stirring.

❈ Add 1/4 cup butter, seafood stock and beer to the shrimp mixture in the skillet and mix well. Cook for 2 minutes or until the shrimp turn pink.

❈ Serve with seasoned rice and French bread. Note: This dish may be prepared several hours ahead and stored, covered, in the refrigerator to allow the flavors to blend.

Yield: 2 servings   *Monica Marthaler*

Shrimp Scampi

1 pound fresh shrimp, peeled, deveined
Salt and pepper to taste
1/2 cup margarine or butter
2 teaspoons Worcestershire sauce
1/4 cup sherry
1 to 2 cloves of garlic, pressed
2 tablespoons lemon juice
1 tablespoon sugar
1/2 cup finely chopped parsley

❊ Season the shrimp with salt and pepper. Melt the margarine in a shallow ovenproof pan over low heat. Mix in the next 5 ingredients. Add the shrimp, spooning the sauce over the shrimp. Broil at low for 8 minutes. Let stand for 15 minutes. Sprinkle with the parsley. Broil at high for 3 minutes. Note: If your oven does not have a high and low broiler setting, broil close to the heat source for high and farther from the heat source for low.

Yield: 4 servings   *Jackie Darby*

Crab Meat and Vegetable Pie

6 ounces crab meat
1/2 cup chopped water chestnuts
8 ounces fresh snow peas, blanched
1 tablespoon soy sauce
1 1/2 cups milk
3/4 cup baking mix
3 eggs
1/2 teaspoon pepper

❊ Combine the crab meat, water chestnuts and snow peas in a bowl; mix well. Spoon into a lightly greased 10-inch pie plate or 2-quart casserole. Sprinkle with the soy sauce. Mix the milk, baking mix, eggs and pepper in a bowl. Spoon over the crab meat mixture. Bake at 400 degrees for 35 minutes or until golden brown. Let stand for 5 minutes before serving.

Yield: 6 servings   *Penny Joiner*

SEAFOOD, CHICKEN AND ARTICHOKE CASSEROLE

2 (14-ounce) cans artichoke hearts, drained
2 pounds crab meat, cooked
4 chicken breasts, cooked, chopped
1½ pounds fresh mushrooms, sliced
2 tablespoons unsalted butter
3 cups White Sauce
1 tablespoon Worcestershire sauce
½ cup sherry
Salt and pepper to taste
½ cup freshly grated Parmesan cheese
1½ cups bread crumbs
Paprika to taste

�֎ Arrange the artichoke hearts in a buttered 9x13-inch glass baking dish. Add the crab meat and chicken. Sauté the mushrooms in the butter in a skillet for 2 minutes; drain well. Spoon the mushrooms over the crab meat and chicken.

✷ Blend the White Sauce, Worcestershire sauce, sherry, salt and pepper in a bowl. Pour over the mushrooms. Sprinkle with the cheese, bread crumbs and paprika.

✷ Bake at 375 degrees for 40 minutes. Serve with hot cooked rice and a green salad. May substitute peeled cooked shrimp for the crab meat.

WHITE SAUCE

¾ cup melted unsalted butter
¾ cup flour
3 cups milk, heated

✷ Combine the butter and flour in a saucepan and mix well. Cook over medium heat until thickened, stirring constantly. Add the milk gradually, stirring constantly until creamy.

Yield: 10 servings

Allison Newton

GRILLED TUNA STEAKS

1 cup water
1 cup soy sauce
1 envelope Italian salad dressing mix
1 cup vegetable oil
4 (1-inch-thick) tuna steaks

❈ Mix the water, soy sauce, salad dressing mix and oil in a shallow dish or pan. Add the steaks. Marinate, covered, in the refrigerator for 30 minutes or longer.

❈ Remove the tuna from the marinade, discarding the marinade. Grill on a grill rack sprayed with nonstick cooking spray for 5 minutes per side.

Yield: 4 servings   *Cindy Tanner*

TARTAR SAUCE

1 cup mayonnaise
1/2 cup sour cream
2 tablespoons prepared mustard
1 onion, finely chopped
1/2 cup dill relish
1/2 cup chopped green olives
1 tablespoon lemon juice
1/4 tablespoon sugar

❈ Combine the mayonnaise, sour cream, mustard, onion, relish, olives, lemon juice and sugar in a bowl and mix well. Chill, covered, for 1 to 2 hours or longer.

Yield: 40 servings   *Allison Newton*

BEEFY TOMATO-STUFFED SHELLS

1 pound ground beef
1/2 cup minced onion
1/2 teaspoon black pepper
1/4 teaspoon garlic powder
1/4 teaspoon crushed red pepper
1 1/4 cups beef broth
1 (7-ounce) jar oil-pack sun-dried tomatoes, drained
1/4 cup toasted almonds
1/4 cup chopped fresh basil leaves
2 tablespoons chopped fresh parsley
2 cloves of garlic, sliced
1/4 cup olive oil
1/3 cup grated Parmesan cheese
24 jumbo macaroni shells, cooked, drained
1 (32-ounce) jar spaghetti sauce
1 1/2 cups shredded mozzarella cheese
1 to 2 tablespoons chopped fresh parsley

❈ Brown the ground beef with the onion in a large skillet, stirring until the ground beef is crumbly; drain well. Add the black pepper, garlic powder and red pepper and mix well. Cover and set aside.

❈ Combine the beef broth, tomatoes, almonds, basil, 2 tablespoons parsley and garlic in a blender container. Process until well mixed. Add the olive oil in a slow stream with the blender running. Process until mixed. Stir the tomato mixture into the ground beef mixture. Stir in the Parmesan cheese. Spoon 1 rounded tablespoonful of the ground beef mixture into each macaroni shell. Arrange the filled macaroni shells in a lightly greased 9x13-inch baking dish or ovenproof serving dish. Pour the spaghetti sauce over the top.

❈ Bake, covered, at 375 degrees for 20 to 30 minutes or until heated through. Sprinkle with the mozzarella cheese. Bake, uncovered, for 5 minutes or until the mozzarella cheese is melted. Sprinkle with 1 to 2 tablespoons parsley.

Yield: 12 servings   *Katherine Bendall*

Lasagna

1 pound ground chuck
1/2 cup chopped onion
1 clove of garlic, chopped
1 (16-ounce) can tomatoes
1 (8-ounce) can tomato sauce
1 (6-ounce) can tomato paste
2 teaspoons crushed dried basil
1 (10-ounce) package frozen spinach, thawed, drained
1 teaspoon salt
1 teaspoon vegetable oil
8 ounces lasagna noodles
2 eggs
2 1/2 cups ricotta cheese
1/2 cup grated Parmesan cheese
2 tablespoons dried parsley flakes
1 teaspoon salt
1/2 teaspoon pepper
1 pound mozzarella cheese, shredded
1/4 cup grated Parmesan cheese

❊ Brown the ground chuck with the onion and garlic in a skillet, stirring until the ground chuck is crumbly; drain well. Stir in the undrained tomatoes, tomato sauce, tomato paste, basil and spinach. Simmer, covered, for 15 minutes, stirring frequently.

❊ Combine the salt, oil and enough water to cover the noodles in a saucepan. Bring to a boil. Drop in the noodles. Cook until tender; drain and rinse well.

❊ Beat the eggs in a bowl. Add the ricotta cheese, 1/2 cup Parmesan cheese, parsley, 1 teaspoon salt and pepper and mix well.

❊ Layer the noodles, ricotta filling, mozzarella cheese and meat sauce 1/2 at a time in a 9x13-inch baking dish. Sprinkle with 1/4 cup Parmesan cheese. Bake at 375 degrees for 30 to 35 minutes or until heated through.

Yield: 10 servings   *Pamela Roberts*

Veal Piccata over Angel Hair Pasta

6 to 8 ounces angel hair pasta
4 veal cutlets
¼ cup flour
½ teaspoon salt
¼ teaspoon pepper
1½ tablespoons peanut oil
3 tablespoons vermouth or white wine
2 tablespoons butter or margarine
2 tablespoons lemon juice

❀ Cook the pasta using the package directions; drain well. Flatten the veal to ⅛-inch thickness between sheets of waxed paper.

❀ Mix the flour, salt and pepper in a shallow dish. Dredge the veal in the flour mixture.

❀ Cook the veal in the peanut oil in a 12-inch skillet for 1 to 2 minutes per side. Remove the veal to a plate; tent with foil to keep warm.

❀ Add the vermouth to the skillet, stirring to scrape up any browned bits. Add the butter and lemon juice and mix well. Cook until the butter is melted, stirring constantly.

❀ Arrange the pasta on serving plates. Top with the veal cutlets. Spoon the sauce over the pasta and veal. Garnish with grated lemon peel and dried basil.

Yield: 2 servings   *Amy Darby*

Marinated Chicken Breasts in Pepper Fettuccini

1/2 cup olive oil
1/2 cup minced fresh basil
3 tablespoons fresh lemon juice
1 tablespoon crushed red pepper flakes
2 teaspoons minced garlic
2 pounds boneless chicken breasts
3/4 cup freshly grated Parmesan cheese
Pepper Sauce
12 ounces spinach fettuccini, cooked, drained

※ Mix the olive oil, 1/4 cup of the basil, lemon juice, pepper flakes and garlic in a shallow dish. Add the chicken, turning to coat. Marinate, covered, in the refrigerator overnight. Drain the chicken, discarding the marinade. Broil or grill the chicken 4 inches from the heat source until cooked through, turning once. Stir the cheese and 1/4 cup basil into hot Pepper Sauce in a bowl. Divide the fettuccini evenly among 8 serving plates. Top with the chicken. Spoon the Pepper Sauce mixture over the top.

Pepper Sauce

3 tablespoons unsalted butter
1 each medium red and yellow bell pepper, julienned
1/2 cup each dry white wine and chicken broth
2 cups whipping cream
1 cup sliced mushrooms
2 tablespoons unsalted butter
1/2 teaspoon salt

※ Melt 3 tablespoons butter in a skillet. Add the peppers. Sauté for 2 minutes. Remove the peppers. Stir the wine and broth into the drippings in the skillet. Boil over high heat for 5 minutes or until reduced to 2 tablespoons. Add the whipping cream. Cook for 4 minutes or until reduced by 1/2. Sauté the mushrooms in 2 tablespoons butter in a skillet over medium-high heat until lightly browned. Mix in the peppers, cream sauce and salt.

Yield: 8 servings   *Beth Cox*

CHICKEN PECAN FETTUCCINI

1/4 cup butter or margarine
1 pound boneless chicken breasts, cut into 3/4-inch pieces
3 cups sliced mushrooms
1 cup sliced green onions
1/4 teaspoon pepper
1/4 teaspoon salt
1/4 teaspoon garlic powder
10 ounces fettuccini
1/2 cup melted butter or margarine
1 egg yolk
2/3 cup half-and-half
2 tablespoons chopped fresh parsley
1/4 teaspoon salt
1/4 teaspoon pepper
1/4 teaspoon garlic powder
1/2 cup grated Parmesan cheese
1 cup toasted chopped pecans

✽ Melt 1/4 cup butter in a large skillet. Add the chicken. Sauté until lightly browned. Remove the chicken and set aside.

✽ Add the mushrooms, green onions, 1/4 teaspoon pepper, 1/4 teaspoon salt and 1/4 teaspoon garlic powder to the skillet. Sauté until the vegetables are tender. Add the chicken and mix well. Simmer for 20 minutes or until the chicken is cooked through, stirring occasionally.

✽ Cook the fettuccini using the package directions; drain well. Combine 1/2 cup butter, egg yolk, half-and-half, parsley, 1/4 teaspoon salt, 1/4 teaspoon pepper and 1/4 teaspoon garlic powder in a medium bowl and mix well. Combine with the fettuccini in a large bowl and mix well. Add the cheese, tossing until mixed. Add the chicken mixture and toss well.

✽ To serve, arrange the chicken and fettuccini mixture on a serving platter. Sprinkle with the pecans. Serve immediately.

Yield: 6 servings   Linda Ray

CHICKEN PASTA

1/3 cup Champagne or white wine
1/4 teaspoon cayenne
2 medium cloves of garlic, minced
1 pound boneless skinless chicken breasts
2 tablespoons olive oil
1 small bell pepper, thinly sliced
1 (15-ounce) can tomato sauce
1/3 cup sliced black olives
1/4 cup grated Parmesan cheese
1/2 teaspoon oregano
1/2 teaspoon chives
1/8 teaspoon basil, or to taste
3 drops of Tabasco sauce, or to taste
8 ounces rotini
1/4 cup shredded mozzarella cheese

❈ Combine the Champagne, cayenne and garlic in a shallow dish. Add the chicken. Marinate, covered, for 10 minutes. Drain the chicken, reserving the marinade.

❈ Cook the chicken in 2 tablespoons olive oil in a large skillet for several minutes. Add the bell pepper. Cook until the chicken is cooked through.

❈ Add the tomato sauce, olives, Parmesan cheese, oregano, chives, basil and Tabasco sauce and mix well. Add the reserved marinade and mix well. Cook for 10 minutes.

❈ Cook the rotini using the package directions; drain well. To serve, arrange the pasta on a serving plate. Add the chicken mixture. Sprinkle with the mozzarella cheese and toss lightly until mixed.

Yield: 4 servings   *Valerie Wesson*

CHICKEN CAPELLINI

1 pound capellini
1 envelope garlic and herb salad dressing mix
8 cups chopped cooked chicken
2 (9-ounce) packages frozen artichoke hearts, cooked, drained
2 (4-ounce) cans sliced pitted black olives, drained
2 cups mayonnaise
1/2 cup chopped parsley
2 cups sliced green onions
1 (8-ounce) can sliced water chestnuts
1 (14-ounce) can hearts of palm, thinly sliced
1 (2-ounce) jar pimento

❀ Cook the pasta just to al dente using the package directions; drain well. Combine the warm pasta and salad dressing mix in a large bowl and toss well. Let cool. Chill, covered, in the refrigerator overnight. Add the chicken, artichoke hearts, olives, mayonnaise, parsley, green onions, water chestnuts, hearts of palm and pimento and mix well. Chill, covered, for 6 hours or longer.

❀ May serve hot or cold. To serve hot, bake at 350 degrees for 20 minutes or until heated through. Recipe may be halved.

Yield: 15 servings   *Kathy Gamble*

JUDY MCKELVEY, EXECUTIVE DIRECTOR OF THE BIG BROTHERS/BIG SISTERS OF THE SHOALS, SAYS, "OUR SERVICE LEAGUE VOLUNTEERS HAVE BEEN LOYAL, HARD-WORKING, AND WILLING TO SERVE IN ANY CAPACITY. WE HAVE ENJOYED THEIR PARTICIPATION AND ALWAYS LOOK FORWARD TO WORKING WITH THEM DURING THE YEAR." ONE PARTICULAR ACTIVITY THAT THE SERVICE LEAGUE SUPPORTS IS BOWLING FOR KIDS SAKE.

Fettuccini Alfredo

1/2 cup butter
1 1/2 cups grated Parmesan cheese
1 cup whipping cream
1/4 cup chopped fresh parsley
12 ounces fettuccini, cooked, drained

❀ Melt the butter in a saucepan over medium heat. Stir in the cheese. Add the whipping cream gradually, stirring after each addition until blended. Cook just to the boiling point, stirring constantly. Remove from the heat. Stir in the parsley. Toss the pasta with the sauce in a bowl. May add grilled chicken or shrimp.

Yield: 6 servings   *Donna Parkes*

Pasta with Broccoli and Mushrooms

1/4 cup olive oil
1 clove of garlic, minced
1/2 bunch broccoli, chopped
7 ounces mushrooms, sliced
1 medium red bell pepper, julienned
1/4 cup each water and dry white wine
8 ounces fettuccini or linguini
1 teaspoon salt
2 tablespoons butter
1/2 cup grated Parmesan cheese

❀ Heat the olive oil in a large skillet over medium heat. Add the next 4 ingredients. Cook for 1 minute, stirring frequently. Discard the garlic once it turns brown. Add the water and wine. Cook, covered, over low heat for 5 minutes or until the broccoli is tender-crisp.

❀ Cook the pasta in a large stockpot of boiling salted water until al dente. Drain the pasta well and return to the stockpot. Toss with the butter. Stir in the broccoli mixture and cheese. Season with salt and pepper if desired.

Yield: 2 servings   *Leigh Ann Morrison*

PENNE PASTA WITH TOMATOES, OLIVES AND TWO CHEESES

3 tablespoons olive oil
1½ cups chopped onions
1 teaspoon minced garlic
3 (28-ounce) cans Italian plum tomatoes, drained
2 teaspoons dried basil
½ teaspoon crushed red pepper
2 cups canned low-sodium chicken broth
Salt and black pepper to taste
1 pound penne or rigatoni pasta
1 teaspoon salt
3 tablespoons olive oil
2½ cups packed shredded Havarti cheese
⅓ cup sliced pitted kalamata olives or other brine-cured olives
⅓ cup grated Parmesan cheese
¼ cup finely chopped fresh basil

✹ Heat 3 tablespoons olive oil in a large heavy Dutch oven over medium-high heat. Add the onions and garlic. Sauté for 5 minutes or until the onions are translucent. Add the tomatoes, dried basil and red pepper; mix well. Bring to a boil, breaking up the tomatoes with the back of a spoon.

✹ Add the chicken broth. Return to a boil; reduce the heat to medium. Simmer for 1 hour or until there is approximately 6 cups sauce, stirring occasionally and continuing to break up the tomatoes with a spoon. Season with salt and black pepper. At this point the sauce may be covered and stored in the refrigerator for up to 2 days. Rewarm over low heat.

✹ Cook the pasta to al dente in boiling salted water in a stockpot using the package directions; drain well. Return the pasta to the stockpot. Add 3 tablespoons olive oil and toss well. Add the sauce, tossing to mix well. Stir in the Havarti cheese. Spoon into a 9x13-inch baking dish.

✹ Sprinkle with the olives and Parmesan cheese. Bake, covered loosely with foil, at 375 degrees for 20 to 30 minutes or until the pasta is heated through. Bake, uncovered, for 2 minutes. Sprinkle with the fresh basil.

Yield: 8 servings   *Teresa Standard*

Vegetables & Side Dishes

TAMBRA HOWARD

TAMBRA HOWARD

Tambra Howard is a native of Muscle Shoals, Alabama, where her husband and two children keep her busy. But she still finds time to teach art to grades kindergarten through seven in the Muscle Shoals City School System. Tambra has degrees in graphic design, visual arts, art history, and art education. She loves bold shapes and bold color, acrylics and oil, and enjoys mixed media. She specializes in hand-painted pottery and ceramics that focus on art history.

Stuffed Artichokes

1/2 cup Italian bread crumbs
1/4 cup grated Parmesan cheese
Garlic salt to taste
2 artichokes, cleaned, trimmed
1 tablespoon (about) olive oil

❀ Mix the bread crumbs, cheese and garlic salt in a bowl. Sprinkle the artichokes with the oil. Stuff with the cheese mixture.

❀ Fit the artichokes snugly into a steamer. Steam in a small amount of water until tender.

Yield: 2 servings   *Melissa Weatherly*

Basic Asparagus Casserole

1 (15-ounce) can asparagus spears
3 tablespoons butter
3 tablespoons flour
1 cup milk
1/2 teaspoon salt
Pepper to taste
1 cup shredded sharp Cheddar cheese
2 hard-cooked eggs, sliced
1/2 cup blanched slivered almonds

❀ Drain the asparagus, reserving 1/2 cup liquid. Melt the butter in a saucepan. Add the flour and blend well. Add the milk and reserved liquid, stirring until smooth. Season with salt and pepper. Add the cheese and mix well. Cook until the cheese is melted, stirring constantly.

❀ Layer the asparagus and eggs in a greased 1 1/2-quart casserole. Spoon the sauce over the top. Sprinkle with the almonds. Bake at 350 degrees for 25 minutes. May add cooked chopped celery or English peas and slivered water chestnuts.

Yield: 8 servings   *Amy Jon Finch*

BAKED BEANS

1 pound ground beef
Salt and pepper to taste
1 medium onion, chopped
1/4 cup chopped bell pepper
1 (30-ounce) can pork and beans
1 cup catsup
2/3 cup packed brown sugar
2 tablespoons each prepared mustard and Worcestershire sauce

✻ Season the ground beef with salt and pepper. Brown the ground beef with the onion and bell pepper in a skillet, stirring until the ground beef is crumbly; drain well. Mix in the remaining ingredients. Spoon into a 2-quart casserole. Bake at 325 degrees for 1 hour.

Yield: 8 servings   *Simone Mitchell*

FRENCH BEAN BUNDLES

1 cup vegetable oil
1/2 cup vinegar
2/3 cup each sugar and catsup
1/2 onion, grated
1 teaspoon salt
Juice of 1/2 lemon
6 (16-ounce) cans French-style green beans, drained
Bacon slices, cut into halves
Paprika to taste

✻ Beat the first 7 ingredients in a bowl. Arrange the green beans in 2-inch bundles; wrap each bundle with 1/2 bacon slice, securing with wooden picks. Place in a baking dish. Pour the vinegar mixture over the bundles. Marinate, covered, in the refrigerator for 4 hours. Bake, covered with foil, at 350 degrees for 1 hour, turning the bundles once. Bake, uncovered, until the bacon is browned and cooked through. Remove the bundles to a serving dish. Spoon the cooking liquid over the bundles. Sprinkle with paprika.

Yield: 12 servings   *Lydia Nolen*

Broccoli Casserole

2 (10-ounce) packages frozen broccoli
1 (10-ounce) can cream of mushroom soup
1 cup shredded Cheddar cheese
1 small onion, chopped
2 eggs, beaten
1/2 cup mayonnaise
1/2 tablespoon salt
1 sleeve butter crackers, crushed
1 tablespoon (about) butter

❈ Cook the broccoli using the package directions; drain well. Combine the broccoli, soup, cheese, onion, eggs, mayonnaise and salt in a bowl and mix well. Spoon into a greased casserole. Top with the cracker crumbs. Dot with the butter. Bake at 350 degrees for 45 minutes. May add one 8-ounce can sliced water chestnuts.

Yield: 8 servings   *Connie Mills*

New Year's Day Sauerkraut

2 pounds sauerkraut, drained
2 cups dry white wine
2 teaspoons seasoned salt
1 teaspoon caraway seeds
5 whole allspice
1/4 cup butter
1/2 cup sour cream
1/2 cup crumbled crisp-cooked bacon

❈ Combine the sauerkraut, wine, seasoned salt, caraway seeds, allspice and butter in a saucepan and mix well. Simmer, covered, for 20 minutes. Top each serving with sour cream and bacon. Serve with black-eyed peas.

Yield: 8 servings   *Amy Holcomb*

Sweet-and-Sour Carrots

2 pounds carrots, sliced
1 cup sugar
1/2 cup vinegar
1/4 cup vegetable oil
1 (10-ounce) can tomato soup
1 teaspoon salt
1 teaspoon pepper
1 teaspoon dry mustard
1 medium green bell pepper, chopped
1 medium onion, chopped

Cook the carrots in water to cover in a saucepan until tender; drain well. Combine the sugar, vinegar, oil, soup, salt, pepper and mustard in a saucepan. Boil for 2 to 3 minutes. Mix the carrots, bell pepper and onion in a large bowl. Pour the sauce over the vegetable mixture and mix well. Chill, covered, overnight. Serve cold or hot.

Yield: 10 servings — *Cindy Ott*

Corn Slaw

3 (12-ounce) cans white Shoe Peg corn
1/2 cup chopped onion
1 bell pepper, chopped
2 carrots, grated
1/2 cup mayonnaise
1/2 cup sour cream
2 teaspoons sugar
Salt and pepper to taste

Mix the corn, onion, bell pepper and carrots in a large bowl. Mix the mayonnaise, sour cream, sugar, salt and pepper in a small bowl. Add the dressing to the corn mixture and mix well. Chill, covered, overnight. Keeps well in the refrigerator.

Yield: 8 servings — *Karen Garner*

FRESH CORN LOAF

2 cups fresh corn kernels
1 cup each chopped tomato, onion and green bell pepper
2 teaspoons salt
1/8 teaspoon cayenne
1 cup each yellow cornmeal and shredded Cheddar cheese
2 eggs, beaten
1/2 cup each evaporated milk and water

❋ Mix the corn, tomato, onion, green pepper, salt, cayenne, cornmeal and cheese in a large bowl. Let stand for 30 minutes. Mix the eggs, evaporated milk and water in a bowl. Mix with the vegetable mixture. Spoon into a greased loaf pan or 2-quart casserole. Bake at 375 degrees for 1 hour. Serve hot or cold.

Yield: 8 servings   *Connie McIlwain*

BAKED CORN WITH SOUR CREAM

3 slices bacon
2 tablespoons each chopped onion and flour
1 cup light sour cream
2 (12-ounce) cans Shoe Peg corn, drained
1/4 teaspoon salt
1 cup crushed butter crackers
2 tablespoons melted light margarine

❋ Fry the bacon in a skillet until crisp; drain well, reserving the drippings. Remove and crumble the bacon. Sauté the onion in the drippings in the skillet until translucent. Stir in the flour. Cook over low heat for 1 minute, stirring constantly. Stir in the sour cream, corn and salt gradually. Cook over low heat until heated through, stirring occasionally; do not boil. Stir in the bacon. Spoon into a greased 2-quart casserole. Sprinkle with a mixture of the cracker crumbs and margarine. Bake at 350 degrees for 25 to 30 minutes or until heated through.

Yield: 8 servings   *Debbie Pool*

Eggplant Parmesan

2 tablespoons flour
1 (1-pound) eggplant, peeled, sliced
⅓ cup egg substitute
2 tablespoons skim milk
⅔ cup Italian bread crumbs
6 cups marinara sauce
1 cup shredded mozzarella cheese
2 tablespoons grated Parmesan cheese

✸ Place the flour in a large zip-top plastic bag. Add the eggplant and shake well to coat. Beat the egg substitute and skim milk in a bowl. Dip the eggplant slices into the egg mixture; dredge in the bread crumbs. Place the eggplant slices on a baking sheet sprayed with nonstick cooking spray. Bake at 400 degrees for 6 to 8 minutes or until beginning to brown. Turn the slices over. Bake for 6 to 8 minutes longer or until tender. Alternate layers of eggplant and marinara sauce in a 9x13-inch baking pan sprayed with nonstick cooking spray until all the eggplant and marinara sauce are used. Top with the cheeses. Bake for 5 minutes or until the cheeses are melted.

Yield: 8 servings, or 4 servings as an entrée   Jane Anne Sherrod

Mushroom Casserole

¼ cup butter or margarine
3 (8-ounce) packages mushrooms, sliced
1½ cups herb-seasoned stuffing mix
2 cups shredded sharp Cheddar cheese
¼ cup butter or margarine
½ cup half-and-half

✸ Melt ¼ cup butter in a large skillet over medium heat. Add the mushrooms. Cook until tender, stirring constantly. Stir in the stuffing mix. Layer the mushroom mixture and cheese ½ at a time in an 8x8-inch baking dish sprayed with nonstick cooking spray. Dot with ¼ cup butter. Pour the half-and-half over the top. Bake at 325 degrees for 30 minutes.

Yield: 6 servings   Virginia Hawkins

VIDALIA DEEP-DISH

1 cup rice
1 to 2 cups water
1/2 cup margarine
6 large Vidalia onions, peeled, coarsely chopped
2 tablespoons parsley
1/4 teaspoon each salt and white pepper
1 cup each shredded Swiss cheese and whipping cream
Paprika to taste

❋ Cook the rice in the water in a saucepan until the rice is tender and the water is absorbed. Melt the margarine in a large saucepan. Add the onions. Cook for 15 minutes, stirring frequently. Add the rice, parsley, salt, pepper, cheese and whipping cream and mix well. Spoon into a 9x13-inch baking dish. Bake, covered, at 350 degrees for 30 minutes. Sprinkle with paprika.

Yield: 8 servings   *Marsha Carter*

HOPPING JOHN

2 cups dried black-eyed peas, rinsed, sorted
12 ounces ham, chopped
1 quart water
1 cup chopped onion
1 teaspoon salt
1/2 teaspoon each pepper and hot sauce
2 cups hot cooked rice
1/2 cup chopped green onions

❋ Place the peas in a Dutch oven with enough water to reach 2 inches above the peas. Bring to a boil and boil for 2 minutes. Remove from the heat. Let stand, covered, for 1 hour; drain well. Combine the ham and 1 quart water in a saucepan. Bring to a boil and boil for 15 minutes. Add the peas; reduce the heat. Simmer, covered, for 45 minutes, stirring occasionally. Add the next 4 ingredients. Return to a boil; reduce the heat. Simmer, covered, for 15 minutes or until the peas are tender. Stir in the rice and green onions.

Yield: 8 servings   *Amy Anderson*

Twice-Baked Potatoes

4 to 6 potatoes
1 cup sour cream
1 (8-ounce) package sour cream and onion dip
1 cup shredded Cheddar cheese

❀ Bake the potatoes in the microwave using the manufacturer's directions. Cut into halves lengthwise and let cool. Scoop the pulp from the potatoes, leaving the shells intact. Mix the sour cream and dip in a small bowl. Add the potato pulp and mix well. Stir in most of the cheese.

❀ Spoon the mixture into the potato shells. Place on a baking sheet. Top with the remaining cheese. Bake at 350 degrees until the cheese is melted.

Yield: 6 servings   *Lucy Cook*

Cheesy Potato Casserole

1 (32-ounce) package frozen hash brown potatoes
2 (10-ounce) cans cream of potato soup
2 cups sour cream
2 cups shredded Cheddar cheese
1 cup grated Parmesan cheese
Pepper to taste

❀ Combine the potatoes, soup, sour cream, Cheddar cheese and Parmesan cheese in a bowl and mix well. Season with pepper.

❀ Spoon the mixture into a greased 9x13-inch baking dish. Bake at 400 degrees for 30 to 45 minutes or until the center is bubbly.

Yield: 12 servings   *Karen Garner*

MARINATED POTATO SLICES

8 red potatoes
1 cup olive oil
1/3 cup red wine vinegar
2 tablespoons Dijon mustard
1/2 teaspoon salt
1/4 teaspoon white pepper

❀ Cook the potatoes in boiling water to cover in a 3-quart saucepan for 8 minutes or until tender; drain and let cool. Cut the potatoes into thin slices and place in a shallow dish.

❀ Combine the olive oil, vinegar, Dijon mustard, salt and pepper in a bowl and mix well. Spoon over the potato slices in the dish. Chill, covered, for 8 hours.

Yield: 8 servings   *Loee Miree*

SCALLOPED POTATOES

5 to 6 large potatoes, peeled, sliced
1 1/2 cups chicken broth
1/2 teaspoon salt
1/4 teaspoon pepper
1 cup shredded Swiss cheese
3 tablespoons grated Parmesan cheese

❀ Combine the potatoes, chicken broth, salt and pepper in a Dutch oven. Bring to a boil; reduce the heat. Simmer, covered, for 5 minutes or just until the potatoes are fork tender. Drain the potatoes, reserving the broth.

❀ Layer the potatoes and Swiss cheese 1/2 at a time in a lightly greased 2-quart casserole. Pour the reserved broth over the top. Sprinkle with the Parmesan cheese. Bake, covered, at 350 degrees for 55 minutes. Bake, uncovered, for 5 minutes or until the potatoes are tender.

Yield: 8 servings   *Kathy Gamble*

CELERY AND GARLIC MASHED POTATOES

5 Idaho baking potatoes, peeled, cut into 2-inch cubes
3 ribs celery, cut into pieces
1/2 cup butter
1 cup whipping cream
2 tablespoons chopped garlic
Salt and pepper to taste

❀ Cook the potatoes and celery in boiling water to cover in a saucepan until the potatoes are tender; drain well. Purée the potato mixture in a food processor. Remove to a mixer bowl and beat until smooth. Add the butter, whipping cream and garlic and beat well. Season with salt and pepper.

Yield: 6 servings   *Sabrina Scarborough*

SPINACH CHEESE BAKE

1 (6-ounce) package corn muffin mix
2 eggs, beaten
2 cups sour cream
1 (10-ounce) can French onion soup
1/2 cup melted butter
1 (10-ounce) package frozen spinach, thawed, drained
1/2 cup shredded Cheddar cheese

❀ Combine the corn muffin mix, eggs, sour cream, soup, butter and spinach in a large bowl and mix well. Spoon into a 2-quart baking dish sprayed with nonstick cooking spray.

❀ Bake at 350 degrees for 25 minutes. Sprinkle with the cheese. Bake for 5 minutes or until the cheese is melted. May use light or low-fat sour cream and cheese in this recipe.

Yield: 8 servings   *Amy Darby*

SPANAKOPITA

1 (1-pound) package frozen phyllo dough
1 tablespoon olive oil
2 cups minced onions
¼ to ½ teaspoon salt
1 teaspoon each basil and oregano
2½ pounds fresh spinach, trimmed, finely chopped
5 medium cloves of garlic, minced
3 tablespoons flour
2 to 3 cups packed crumbled feta cheese
1 cup cottage cheese
Pepper to taste
⅓ to ½ cup olive oil

❁ Thaw the phyllo dough completely in the package. Do not unwrap until ready to use; keep the unused phyllo covered until needed.

❁ For the filling, heat 1 tablespoon olive oil in a Dutch oven. Add the onions, salt, basil and oregano. Sauté for 5 minutes or until the onions are tender. Add the spinach; increase the heat. Cook for 5 to 8 minutes or until the spinach wilts, stirring constantly. Stir in the garlic. Sprinkle in the flour. Cook over medium heat for 2 to 3 minutes or until smooth, stirring constantly. Remove from the heat. Stir in the feta cheese and cottage cheese. Adjust the seasonings, adding generous amounts of pepper.

❁ To assemble, fit 1 sheet of phyllo dough into a lightly oiled 9x13-inch baking pan, allowing the edges of the dough to go up the sides of the pan. Brush lightly with some of the ⅓ to ½ cup olive oil. Repeat this process until there are 8 layers of dough in the pan. Spoon half the filling onto the phyllo in the pan, spreading to the edges. Add 8 more layers of phyllo dough, brushing each sheet lightly with olive oil. Top with the remaining filling. Layer the remaining phyllo dough on top, brushing each sheet lightly with olive oil. Fold over and tuck in the overhanging sides and ends of the dough.

❁ Bake at 375 degrees for 45 minutes or until golden brown and crispy. Cut into squares to serve.

Yield: 8 servings   *Tonya Southall*

COUNTRY CLUB SQUASH

2 pounds yellow squash, sliced
½ cup chopped onion
½ cup boiling water
1 cup sour cream
½ teaspoon salt
¼ teaspoon pepper
¼ teaspoon dried whole basil
1 cup soft bread crumbs
½ cup shredded medium Cheddar cheese
⅓ cup melted butter or margarine
½ teaspoon paprika
8 slices bacon, crisp-cooked, crumbled

❈ Cook the squash and onion in the boiling water in a saucepan until tender; drain well and mash. Combine the squash mixture, sour cream, salt, pepper and basil in a bowl and mix well. Spoon into a greased 2-quart casserole.

❈ Mix the bread crumbs, cheese, butter and paprika in a bowl. Sprinkle over the squash mixture. Top with the crumbled bacon. Bake at 300 degrees for 20 minutes.

Yield: 6 servings

Lynne Bevis

ACCORDING TO MUSCLE SHOALS OFFICE COORDINATOR PAM LONGCRIER, RN, "CHILDREN'S REHABILITATION SERVICE [ALABAMA DEPARTMENT OF REHABILITATION SERVICES] HAS DEPENDED UPON THE SERVICE LEAGUE FOR A NUMBER OF YEARS FOR SEVERAL ONGOING CONTRIBUTIONS. THE SERVICE LEAGUE HAS A TRANSPORTATION FUND SET UP FOR OUR FAMILIES WHO MUST TRAVEL TO HUNTSVILLE OR BIRMINGHAM TO OBTAIN SPECIALIZED MEDICAL CARE NOT PROVIDED LOCALLY. THE LEAGUE ALSO PROVIDES A WONDERFUL CHRISTMAS PARTY FOR OUR CHILDREN ATTENDING CLINIC IN MUSCLE SHOALS. ALL THE LEAGUE MEMBERS WE HAVE WORKED WITH HAVE A GENUINE CONCERN FOR THE FAMILIES SERVED BY OUR AGENCY. WE ARE VERY APPRECIATIVE OF THE SERVICE LEAGUE."

Zucchini Toss

1 tablespoon olive oil
4 to 6 zucchini, cut into bite-size pieces
2 tablespoons lemon juice
1 tablespoon grated Parmesan cheese
1 teaspoon lemon pepper

❋ Heat the olive oil in a skillet. Add the zucchini. Cook until tender-crisp, stirring frequently. Remove from the heat. Let stand, covered, for 5 minutes. Sprinkle the zucchini with the lemon juice. Add a mixture of the cheese and lemon pepper and toss to mix. Serve immediately.

Yield: 6 servings   *Joann Campbell*

Vegetables and Dill

2 small zucchini, thinly sliced
2 small yellow squash, thinly sliced
3 medium tomatoes, cut into quarters
1 (6-ounce) jar marinated artichoke hearts, drained, sliced
1 tablespoon minced fresh dill, or 1 teaspoon dillweed
2 teaspoons lemon juice
1/2 teaspoon salt
1/4 teaspoon sugar

❋ Place the zucchini and squash slices in a nonstick 12-inch skillet. Top with the tomatoes and artichoke hearts. Sprinkle with the dill, lemon juice, salt and sugar. Cook over medium heat for 20 to 30 minutes or until the vegetables are tender, stirring occasionally.

Yield: 6 servings   *Melissa Weatherly*

VEGETABLE CASSEROLE

1 (12-ounce) can white Shoe Peg corn, drained
1 (16-ounce) can French-style green beans, drained
1/2 cup each chopped onion and chopped celery
1 (2-ounce) jar pimento, drained
1/2 cup shredded Cheddar cheese
1/2 cup sour cream
1 (10-ounce) can cream of celery soup
1/2 teaspoon each salt and pepper
1/4 cup melted margarine
1 cup butter cracker crumbs

❈ Mix the corn, green beans, onion, celery, pimento, cheese, sour cream, soup, salt and pepper in a bowl. Spoon into a 2-quart casserole.

❈ Top with a mixture of the margarine and cracker crumbs. Bake at 350 degrees for 45 minutes. May add 1/2 cup slivered almonds to the topping.

Yield: 8 servings   *Karen Garner*

MACARONI CASSEROLE

1 (8-ounce) package macaroni
1 pound sharp Cheddar cheese, shredded
1 (10-ounce) can cream of mushroom soup
1 cup mayonnaise
1 cup chopped onion
1/4 cup chopped green bell pepper
1/4 cup pimento

❈ Combine the macaroni, cheese, soup, mayonnaise, onion, green pepper and pimento in a bowl and mix well. Spoon into a 2-quart casserole. Bake at 350 degrees for 40 minutes. May add 8 ounces sliced mushrooms and 1/2 teaspoon Worcestershire sauce.

Yield: 8 servings   *Pam Clepper*

Consommé Rice Casserole

1 cup rice
1 cup water
½ cup margarine
⅓ cup chopped onion
1 (10-ounce) can cream of mushroom soup
1 (10-ounce) can beef consommé

✽ Combine the rice and water in a casserole. Bake at 325 degrees until the water is absorbed. Add the remaining ingredients and mix well. Bake, covered, at 325 degrees for 30 minutes. Bake, uncovered, for 25 minutes.

Yield: 8 servings   *Jackie Stutts*

Dirty Rice

1 (3-pound) chicken
1 pound ground sausage
2 medium onions, chopped
1 bell pepper, chopped
4 ribs celery, chopped
2 cloves of garlic, chopped
1 (2-ounce) jar pimento, drained
3 cups cooked wild rice

✽ Cook the chicken in water to cover in a stockpot until tender; drain well, reserving the broth. Chop the chicken, discarding the skin and bones.

✽ Brown the sausage in a skillet, stirring until crumbly. Add the onions, bell pepper, celery and garlic and mix well. Cook until the vegetables are tender, stirring occasionally; drain well.

✽ Mix the chicken, reserved broth, pimento, sausage mixture and rice in a large bowl. Spoon into a 9x13-inch baking dish. Bake at 350 degrees for 45 minutes.

Yield: 8 servings   *Joni Lumpkin*

YORKSHIRE PUDDING

1 cup flour
1/2 teaspoon salt
2 eggs
1 cup milk
1/4 cup beef drippings

❋ Sift the flour and salt together. Beat the eggs and milk in a bowl. Add the flour mixture and beat with a whisk just until smooth and blended; do not overbeat.

❋ Pour the beef drippings into a heated soufflé dish. Bake at 450 degrees for 10 minutes. Reduce the oven temperature to 350 degrees. Bake for 10 to 15 minutes or until puffy and browned. Serve with roast beef.

Yield: 6 servings   *Sarah Perry*

BROWN'S RELISH

2 1/2 gallons tomatoes
8 very large bell peppers, finely chopped
8 very large onions, finely chopped
12 to 15 jalapeños, finely chopped
3 cups vinegar
4 pounds sugar

❋ Peel the tomatoes and chop finely. Strain the juice and reserve for another use. Combine the tomatoes, bell peppers, onions, jalapeños, vinegar and sugar in a large stockpot and mix well. Simmer for 1 to 2 hours or until of desired consistency.

❋ Ladle the relish into 8 to 10 hot sterilized pint jars, leaving 1/2 inch headspace; seal with 2-piece lids. Process in a boiling water bath for 10 minutes. Spread over cream cheese for an appetizer or use as hot dog relish.

Yield: 80 servings   *Lydia Nolen*

Desserts & Sweet Snacks

ANDREA GREENE

ANDREA GREENE

Andrea Greene began painting, as most artists do, before she learned to write. Since graduating with a degree in art, she has gone on to exhibit her work in different galleries across the South. She has painted professionally for over twenty years and applies this experience in creating murals, hand-painted furniture, and oil paintings. Each work is truly an original, thus the name "Annie's Originals."

BU'S APPLE DUMPLINGS

10 homemade or canned buttermilk biscuits
1 cup raisins
5 medium apples, peeled, cored, cut into halves
2/3 cup sugar
2/3 cup water
1/3 cup melted butter
2/3 teaspoon vanilla extract
1/4 teaspoon cinnamon
1/4 teaspoon ground cloves
1 tablespoon lemon juice
1 tablespoon cornstarch

❀ Flatten each biscuit into a 6-inch circle. Place 1 spoonful of raisins in each of the cavities created by coring the apples. Wrap 1 biscuit around each apple half. Place the apples seam side down in a greased 9x13-inch glass baking dish.

❀ Combine the sugar, water, butter, vanilla, cinnamon, cloves, lemon juice and cornstarch in a saucepan. Cook until thickened, stirring constantly. Pour over the dumplings.

❀ Bake at 350 degrees for 35 to 40 minutes or until golden brown. Serve warm, plain or with vanilla ice cream.

Yield: 10 servings   *Mary Brook Albritton*

SERVICE LEAGUE MEMBERS SET UP, STAFF, AND OPERATE THE CHILDREN'S ART TENT FOR THE ANNUAL ARTS ALIVE FESTIVAL. AFTER BEING INSPIRED BY SEEING ALL THE ART IN THE PARK, THE CHILDREN COME TO THE TENT TO "MAKE ART" RIGHT AT THE FESTIVAL—AND FUTURE ARTISTS ARE BORN.

BANANA SPLIT CAKE

2 cups graham cracker crumbs
¼ cup melted butter
2 eggs
½ cup butter, softened
2 cups confectioners' sugar
5 bananas, cut into halves lengthwise
1 (15-ounce) jar crushed pineapple
16 ounces whipped topping
1 cup chopped pecans
1 (4-ounce) jar maraschino cherries

✳ Spread the graham cracker crumbs in a 9x13-inch dish. Pour ¼ cup butter over the graham cracker crumbs. Combine the eggs, ½ cup butter and confectioners' sugar in a mixer bowl. Beat for 10 minutes. Spread over the graham cracker crumbs. Top with the bananas and pineapple. Spread with the whipped topping. Top with the pecans and cherries. Note: To avoid any risk of salmonella, replace the eggs with an equivalent amount of egg substitute.

Yield: 15 servings   *Deirdre Kennedy*

BANANAS FOSTER

¼ cup butter
6 tablespoons (rounded) brown sugar
4 bananas, cut into halves or quarters
1 tablespoon each banana liqueur and light rum
2 tablespoons brandy
3 cups vanilla ice cream

✳ Combine the butter and brown sugar in a skillet. Cook over medium heat until the sugar is dissolved, stirring constantly. Add the bananas. Cook until tender. Stir in the liqueur. Sprinkle with the rum and brandy. Remove from the heat and ignite. Spoon the liquid gently over the bananas after the flame subsides. Spoon over each serving of ice cream while warm.

Yield: 6 servings   *Caroline McNeilly*

MINI BLINTZES

2 (16-ounce) loaves white bread
16 ounces cream cheese, softened
2 egg yolks
1/2 cup sugar
1 cup melted butter
1 cup cinnamon sugar

❋ Trim the crusts from the bread. Roll the bread slices flat and set aside.

❋ Combine the cream cheese, egg yolks and sugar in a large bowl and mix well. Spread evenly over 1 side of the bread slices. Roll up as for jelly rolls. Dip each roll into the melted butter; coat each roll with cinnamon sugar. Freeze the rolls on a baking sheet.

❋ Cut each frozen roll into thirds and place on a baking sheet. Bake at 400 degrees for 15 minutes. Serve hot.

Yield: 120 servings   *Mary Armstrong*

THE MISSION OF THE BOYS & GIRLS CLUBS OF NORTHWEST ALABAMA IS TO ASSURE AND ENHANCE THE QUALITY OF LIFE FOR YOUTH AGES 6 THROUGH 18. WITH EMPHASIS ON DISADVANTAGED, AT-RISK YOUTH, THE CLUB OFFERS A DIVERSIFIED DAILY PROGRAM OF PERSONAL AND EDUCATIONAL DEVELOPMENT, LEADERSHIP AND CITIZENSHIP, CULTURAL ENRICHMENT, OUTDOOR AND ENVIRONMENTAL AWARENESS, HEALTH AND PHYSICAL EDUCATION, AND SOCIAL RECREATION TO HELP YOUTHS MATURE INTO HEALTHY, CONTRIBUTING ADULTS. EXECUTIVE DIRECTOR RICHARD A. INCONTRO TELLS US THAT "THE SERVICE LEAGUE HAS BEEN A FRIEND TO THE CLUB SINCE 1991. OUR NEWEST CLUB WAS OPENED IN 1995, AND THE LEAGUE WAS THERE TO HELP US WITH SUPPLIES AND EQUIPMENT TO GET STARTED. TODAY OVER 200 CHILDREN ARE SERVED BY THIS CLUB, AND A RECENT GRANT FROM MSDSL IS HELPING TO EXPAND OUR COMPUTER LAB, WHICH IS AN ESSENTIAL FEATURE IN MAKING OUR KIDS ACADEMICALLY PREPARED. THANKS TO THE GENEROSITY AND CONCERN OF THE MUSCLE SHOALS DISTRICT SERVICE LEAGUE, THE BOYS & GIRLS CLUB IS 'THE POSITIVE PLACE FOR KIDS!'"

CHERRY CHIFFON DESSERT

1 (21-ounce) can cherry pie filling, chilled
1 (15-ounce) can juice-pack pineapple chunks or
    crushed pineapple, drained, chilled
1 (14-ounce) can sweetened condensed milk
8 ounces whipped topping
1 cup miniature marshmallows

❋ Combine the pie filling, pineapple, condensed milk, whipped topping and marshmallows in a bowl and mix well. Spoon into individual dessert bowls or a large serving bowl. Chill, covered, for 30 minutes. Refrigerate any leftovers.

Yield: 10 servings   *Betty Collignon*

CHESS SQUARES

1 (2-layer) package yellow cake mix
1/2 cup margarine, softened
1 egg
8 ounces cream cheese, softened
1 (16-ounce) package confectioners' sugar
2 eggs

❋ Combine the cake mix, margarine and 1 egg in a bowl and mix well; the batter will be thick. Spread in a 10x14-inch baking pan.

❋ Mix the cream cheese, confectioners' sugar and 2 eggs in a bowl. Spread over the cake mix mixture. Bake at 350 degrees for 30 minutes. Cool in the pan. Cut into squares to serve.

Yield: 20 servings   *JoAnne Horton*

MOTHER'S CHOCOLATE FLUFF

1 cup flour
¹/₂ cup butter
8 ounces cream cheese, softened
1 cup confectioners' sugar
16 ounces whipped topping
1 (6-ounce) package chocolate instant pudding mix
1 (6-ounce) package vanilla instant pudding mix
4 cups milk
4 ounces semisweet chocolate
1 cup finely chopped pecans

❊ For the first layer, mix the flour and butter in a bowl. Spread over the bottom of a 3-quart baking dish. Bake at 350 degrees for 20 minutes. Let stand until cool.

❊ For the second layer, combine the cream cheese, confectioners' sugar and 1 cup of the whipped topping in a mixer bowl and beat until smooth. Spread over the cooled crust.

❊ For the third layer, combine the pudding mixes and milk in a mixer bowl and beat until smooth. Spread over the cream cheese layer.

❊ Spread the remaining whipped topping over the pudding layer. Grate the chocolate over the top. Sprinkle with the pecans. Chill, covered, until serving time. Cut into squares to serve.

Yield: 12 servings   *Lisa Trousdale*

CREAM CHEESE PASTRY

2 (8-count) cans refrigerator crescent rolls
½ cup sugar
16 ounces cream cheese, softened
1 egg yolk
1 cup confectioners' sugar
2 to 3 tablespoons milk

❊ Unroll 1 can of the roll dough. Fit into a 9x13-inch glass baking dish, pressing to seal the perforations. Cream the sugar, cream cheese and egg yolk in a mixer bowl until light and fluffy. Spread over the roll dough in the baking dish.

❊ Unroll the remaining dough. Place over the cream cheese mixture, spreading and stretching the dough to each side of the baking dish; press to seal the perforations. Bake at 350 degrees for 8 to 10 minutes or until golden brown. Let stand until cool.

❊ Mix the confectioners' sugar with enough of the milk to make of glaze consistency. Drizzle over the pastry. Cut into small squares to serve.

Yield: 15 servings   *Kaye Mason*

FROM NINA B. WILLIAMS, PROGRAM DIRECTOR OF THE COMMUNITY ACTION AGENCY, COMES THIS MESSAGE: "THE MEALS ON WHEELS PROGRAM APPRECIATES THE SERVICE LEAGUE AND THE CONTRIBUTION YOU HAVE MADE TO THE PROGRAM THROUGHOUT THE YEARS. THE FUNDS THAT HAVE BEEN CONTRIBUTED FEED A NEEDY PERSON IN COLBERT COUNTY AND ONE IN LAUDERDALE COUNTY FOR ONE YEAR. WITHOUT THE ASSISTANCE OF THE SERVICE LEAGUE MEMBERS, OUR PROGRAM WOULD NOT BE THE SUCCESS IT IS TODAY. IT TAKES MORE THAN JUST GIVING ON A MONETARY BASIS TO HAVE A PROGRAM SUCCEED. IT TAKES INDIVIDUALS WHO HAVE A CARING HEART AND SENSE OF PRIDE FOR THEIR COMMUNITY. THIS HAS BEEN PASSED DOWN FROM GENERATION TO GENERATION IN THE SERVICE LEAGUE. THANK YOU FOR YOUR CONTINUED SUPPORT IN THE PROGRAM."

Fruit Pizza

1/4 cup butter or margarine, softened
1/4 cup shortening
3/4 cup sugar
1 egg
1 cup plus 6 tablespoons flour
1 teaspoon cream of tartar
1/2 teaspoon baking soda
1/8 teaspoon salt
1/2 cup sugar
8 ounces cream cheese, softened
Sliced fresh fruit or well drained canned fruit
1/3 (21-ounce) can blueberry pie filling

❖ Cream the butter, shortening, 3/4 cup sugar and egg in a mixer bowl until light and fluffy. Add the flour, cream of tartar, baking soda and salt and mix well. Shape and fit into a greased pizza pan. Bake at 350 degrees for 15 minutes or until lightly browned.

❖ Cream 1/2 cup sugar and cream cheese in a mixer bowl until light and fluffy. Spread over the cooled crust.

❖ Top with the fruit. Spread with the pie filling. May substitute lemon pie filling for the blueberry for a lighter dessert.

Yield: 8 servings *Karran Phillips*

PEACH COBBLER

1/2 cup melted butter
1 cup flour
1 cup sugar
1 cup milk
1 (16-ounce) can peaches

❈ Combine the butter, flour, sugar and milk in a medium bowl and mix well. Spoon over the undrained peaches in a baking pan. Bake at 325 degrees for 30 to 45 minutes or until the cobbler is golden brown. Serve hot with ice cream.

Yield: 4 servings   Stacy Hollaway

NUTTY PEACH CRISP

1 (32-ounce) can syrup-pack peaches
1 (2-layer) package yellow cake mix
1 cup melted butter or margarine
1 cup flaked coconut
1/2 cup chopped pecans
1 pint vanilla ice cream

❈ Place the undrained peaches in a 9x12-inch baking dish. Cover with the cake mix. Loosen any clumps of cake mix but do not stir. Spoon the melted butter over the cake mix. Top with the coconut and pecans. Bake at 325 degrees for 50 to 60 minutes. Serve warm topped with the ice cream.

Yield: 7 servings   Kenda Rusevlyan

Punch Bowl Cake

1 (2-layer) package butter-recipe yellow cake mix
2 (4-ounce) packages vanilla instant pudding mix
4 cups milk
1 (7-ounce) package flaked coconut
2 (21-ounce) cans cherry pie filling
2 (20-ounce) cans crushed pineapple, drained
16 ounces whipped topping

※ Prepare and bake the cake mix using the package directions for a 9x13-inch cake pan. Cool in the pan. Prepare the pudding mix with the milk using the package directions.

※ Crumble half the cake into a punch bowl or 2 large bowls. Add layers of half the pudding, coconut, pie filling and pineapple. Crumble the remaining cake over the pineapple in the punch bowl. Add layers of the remaining pudding, coconut, pie filling and pineapple. Top with the whipped topping. Garnish with cherries and finely chopped pecans. Chill, covered, until serving time.

Yield: 30 servings   *Lynne Bevis*

THE AMERICAN RED CROSS ADAPTED AQUATICS PROGRAM BEGAN DURING WORLD WAR II AS THE CONVALESCENT SWIMMING PROGRAM FOR REHABILITATION OF DISABLED VETERANS. THIS PROGRAM HAS EXPANDED TO INCLUDE THE ENTIRE COMMUNITY OF HANDICAPPED PARTICIPANTS. THROUGH SWIMMING, THE STUDENTS INCREASE THEIR PHYSICAL STRENGTH, COORDINATION, AND CIRCULATION, ALL THE WHILE IMPROVING THEIR SOCIAL SKILLS BY EXPERIENCING SUCCESS, MEETING CHALLENGES, AND LEARNING TO WORK WITH OTHERS. THE LEAGUE HAS PROVIDED VOLUNTEERS AND FUNDED THIS PROGRAM SINCE IT BEGAN HERE IN THE SHOALS IN EARLY 1980, ALLOWING THE AMERICAN RED CROSS OF NORTHWEST ALABAMA TO SERVE NUMEROUS HANDICAPPED INDIVIDUALS OF LAUDERDALE AND COLBERT COUNTIES AND TO OPERATE AS ONE OF THE STATE'S FEW ADAPTED AQUATICS PROGRAMS.

Snow on the Mountain

1 (12-ounce) can evaporated milk
1 (16-ounce) package chocolate chip cookies
32 ounces whipped topping
Fudge Topping

❈ Pour the evaporated milk into a bowl. Dip the cookies 1 at a time in the evaporated milk.

❈ Line a 9x13-inch pan with half the cookies. Top with half the whipped topping.

❈ Repeat the layers of cookies and whipped topping. Freeze, covered, until firm. Cut into squares to serve. Top with warm Fudge Topping.

Fudge Topping

2 cups confectioners' sugar
3 tablespoons baking cocoa
1 (5-ounce) can evaporated milk
1/2 cup margarine

❈ Combine the confectioners' sugar, baking cocoa, evaporated milk and margarine in a saucepan. Cook for 5 minutes. May be stored in a covered glass jar in the refrigerator until needed; reheat in the microwave.

Yield: 24 servings   *Carolyn Wright*

Martha's Blueberry Pecan Cheesecake

¹/₂ cup chopped pecans
2 (9-inch) frozen deep-dish pie shells, thawed
¹/₂ cup confectioners' sugar
8 ounces cream cheese, softened
1 (21-ounce) can blueberry pie filling
16 ounces whipped topping

❈ Press the pecans into the pie shells. Bake at 400 degrees for 10 minutes. Let stand until cool.

❈ Cream the confectioners' sugar and cream cheese in a mixer bowl until light and fluffy. Spread over the cooled crusts. Spread the pie filling over the cream cheese mixture. Chill until set. Top with the whipped topping. Chill for 1 hour before serving.

Yield: 12 servings   Mary Brook Albritton

Erich H. Sigle, Director of Colbert-Lauderdale Attention Home, Inc., recalls, "The Service League provided the seed money to establish our program in 1974. We are proud to say that twenty-three years and thousands of children later, the Service League and the Attention Home Program are still indeed thriving! There have been so many needs that your organization has met in assisting us in providing services to the at-risk and disadvantaged children of our communities. You have purchased vehicles, furniture, carpeting, paint, wallpaper, bedding, supplies, appliances, and so forth. In essence, you have helped purchase the homes and almost everything in them!"

CHOCOLATE CHEESECAKE

16 ounces low-fat cream cheese, softened
1/2 cup sugar
1/2 teaspoon vanilla extract
2 eggs
4 ounces German's sweet chocolate, melted, slightly cooled
1 (9-inch) chocolate crumb pie shell

❈ Beat the cream cheese, sugar and vanilla at medium speed in a mixer bowl until blended. Beat in the eggs. Mix 1 cup of the batter with the melted chocolate in a medium bowl. Spoon the chocolate batter into the pie shell. Top with the plain batter. Bake at 350 degrees for 40 minutes or until the center is almost set. Let cool. Chill for 3 hours to overnight.

Yield: 8 servings   *Lisa Mathews*

CHOCOLATE CHIP CHEESECAKE

8 ounces cream cheese, softened
1/3 cup sugar
1 cup sour cream
2 teaspoons vanilla extract
8 ounces whipped topping
1 cup miniature chocolate chips
1 (9-inch) chocolate crumb or graham cracker pie shell

❈ Beat the cream cheese in a mixer bowl until smooth. Beat in the sugar gradually. Blend in the sour cream and vanilla. Fold in the whipped topping. Stir in the chocolate chips. Spoon into the pie shell. Chill for 4 hours or longer. Garnish with additional chocolate chips.

Yield: 8 servings   *Rhonda Tyree*

"M & M" Cheesecake Squares

1/2 cup margarine, softened
1/3 cup packed brown sugar
1 cup flour
1/2 cup chopped walnuts
1/4 cup sugar
8 ounces cream cheese, softened
1 teaspoon vanilla extract
1 egg
3/4 cup "M & M's" Chocolate Candies

❋ Beat the margarine and brown sugar in a mixer bowl until light and fluffy. Add the flour and walnuts and mix until crumbly. Reserve 1/2 cup of the crumb mixture.

❋ Press the remaining crumb mixture over the bottom of an 8x8-inch baking pan. Bake at 350 degrees for 10 minutes.

❋ Beat the sugar, cream cheese and vanilla at medium speed in a mixer bowl until blended. Add the egg and mix well.

❋ Sprinkle 1/2 cup of the candy over the baked crust. Top with the cream cheese mixture. Chop the remaining 1/4 cup candy and mix with the reserved crumb mixture. Sprinkle over the cream cheese mixture. Bake at 350 degrees for 20 minutes. Let cool before cutting into squares. Chill until serving time.

Yield: 16 servings   *Leigh Ann Morrison*

Spring Breeze Cheesecake

8 ounces cream cheese, softened
1/3 cup sugar
1 cup sour cream
2 teaspoons vanilla extract
8 ounces whipped topping
1 (9-inch) graham cracker pie shell

Beat the cream cheese in a mixer bowl until smooth. Add the sugar gradually, beating after each addition. Blend in the sour cream and vanilla. Fold in the whipped topping. Spoon into the pie shell. Chill for 4 hours or until set. Garnish with fresh berries.

Yield: 8 servings *Cindy Tanner*

Apple Pudding

5 apples, peeled, thinly sliced
3 slices pineapple, chopped
1/4 cup pineapple juice
1/4 cup red cinnamon candies
1/8 teaspoon salt
2 tablespoons flour
3/4 cup sugar
3/4 cup flour
1/8 teaspoon salt
6 tablespoons butter

Mix the apples, pineapple, pineapple juice, candy, 1/8 teaspoon salt and 2 tablespoons flour in a bowl. Spoon into a greased casserole. Combine the sugar, 3/4 cup flour and 1/8 teaspoon salt in a bowl. Cut in the butter until fine crumbs form. Sprinkle over the apple mixture. Bake at 400 degrees for 40 minutes.

Yield: 8 servings *Nan Gardiner*

Lemon Soufflé with Raspberry Sauce

2 envelopes unflavored gelatin
1/2 cup cold water
2/3 cup fresh lemon juice
6 eggs
11/2 cups sugar
2 cups whipping cream, whipped
1 tablespoon grated lemon peel
Raspberry Sauce

❋ Tie a collar of waxed paper around a 11/2-quart soufflé dish. Sprinkle the gelatin over the cold water in a saucepan. Let stand for 20 minutes or until softened. Cook over low heat until the gelatin dissolves, stirring constantly. Let stand until cool. Blend in the lemon juice.

❋ Beat the eggs and sugar in a mixer bowl until thick and pale yellow. Blend in the gelatin mixture. Fold in the whipped cream. Reserve a small amount of the lemon peel for a topping. Fold the remaining lemon peel into the mixture.

❋ Spoon into the prepared soufflé dish. Chill overnight. Remove the collar. Serve with warm or cold Raspberry Sauce. Top with the reserved lemon peel. Note: To avoid any risk of salmonella, replace the eggs with an equivalent amount of egg substitute.

Raspberry Sauce

1/2 cup raspberry jam
2 tablespoons sugar
1/2 cup water

❋ Bring the jam, sugar and water to a boil in a saucepan, stirring constantly. Boil for 2 minutes, stirring constantly. May add kirsch or almond or vanilla extract if desired.

Yield: 12 servings   *Jackie Darby*

White Chocolate Crème Brûlée

4 egg yolks, at room temperature
1/3 cup sugar
2 cups whipping cream
4 ounces white chocolate, chopped
1/2 teaspoon vanilla extract
4 teaspoons brown sugar

❀ Whisk the egg yolks with the sugar in a large bowl until smooth and well mixed.

❀ Bring the whipping cream to a simmer in a 2-quart saucepan over medium-high heat. Add the white chocolate and remove from the heat. Whip until the white chocolate is melted.

❀ Add the white chocolate mixture to the egg yolk mixture 1/2 cup at a time, whisking constantly until smooth. Stir in the vanilla.

❀ Spoon the custard into 4 ramekins. Place the ramekins in a 9x13-inch baking dish or broiler pan. Add enough water to reach 1 to 1 1/2 inches up the side of the ramekins.

❀ Bake at 300 degrees for 45 minutes. May be served warm or at room temperature or may be chilled overnight.

❀ Just before serving time, sprinkle 1 teaspoon of the brown sugar over each custard. Broil for 3 to 5 minutes or until the brown sugar caramelizes.

Yield: 4 servings   *Amy Darby*

LEMON VELVET ICE CREAM

5 to 6 lemons
3 eggs
3 cups sugar
2 cups milk
1 cup whipping cream
2 cups evaporated milk

❋ Juice the lemons and scoop out the pulp. Beat the eggs and sugar in a mixer bowl until creamy. Add the lemon juice, lemon pulp, milk, whipping cream and evaporated milk and mix well. Pour into an ice cream freezer container. Freeze using the manufacturer's directions. May add yellow food coloring. Recipe may be doubled, leaving the amount of milk at 2 cups. May add grated lemon peel.

Yield: 12 servings   *Amy Holcomb*

LIME SORBET

3 cups water
1 cup sugar
2 (6-ounce) cans frozen limeade concentrate
3 cups water

❋ Bring 3 cups water and sugar to a boil in a saucepan, stirring until the sugar dissolves. Set aside. Blend the limeade concentrate with 3 cups water in a blender. Add to the sugar mixture and mix well. Spoon into a 9x13-inch pan. Freeze until semi-firm. Cut into small pieces. Process in a blender until smooth and fluffy. Return to the pan. Freeze until firm. Serve with an ice cream scoop.

Yield: 24 servings   *Joann Campbell*

GRANDMOTHER'S PEACH ICE CREAM

2½ cups mashed peeled fresh peaches
2½ cups sugar
Juice of ½ lemon
2 cups whipping cream
1 quart milk
1 (12-ounce) can evaporated milk

❋ Mix the peaches, sugar and lemon juice in a medium bowl. Mix the whipping cream, milk and evaporated milk in a large bowl. Add the peach mixture and mix well. Pour into an ice cream freezer container. Freeze using the manufacturer's directions.

Yield: 15 servings   *Joanna Hardwick*

HOMEMADE VANILLA ICE CREAM

6 medium eggs, beaten
2 cups plus 6 tablespoons sugar
4 cups milk
2 cups half-and-half
3 cups whipping cream
¼ teaspoon salt
2¼ tablespoons vanilla extract

❋ Beat the eggs and sugar in a bowl. Add the milk, half-and-half, whipping cream, salt and vanilla and beat well. Pour into an ice cream freezer container. Freeze using the manufacturer's directions.

❋ Note: To avoid the risk of salmonella, you may wish to use an equivalent amount of pasteurized egg substitute in this recipe, or heat the eggs and approximately ¾ cup of the milk to 160 degrees in a saucepan before proceeding with the recipe.

Yield: 12 servings   *Alison Pigg*

White Chocolate and Macadamia Nut Cookies

1 cup flour
3/4 teaspoon baking powder
1/8 teaspoon salt
1/8 teaspoon baking soda
1/2 cup plus 2 tablespoons unsalted butter, softened
3/4 cup packed light brown sugar
1 teaspoon vanilla extract
1 egg
1 1/2 cups white chocolate chips
3/4 cup coarsely chopped macadamia nuts
3/4 cup coarsely chopped pecans

❋ Mix the flour, baking powder, salt and baking soda together and set aside.

❋ Cream the butter, brown sugar and vanilla in a mixer bowl until light and fluffy. Beat in the egg.

❋ Add the flour mixture to the creamed mixture gradually, beating well after each addition. Add the white chocolate chips, macadamia nuts and pecans, stirring to mix well.

❋ Drop by spoonfuls onto greased cookie sheets. Bake at 350 degrees for 15 minutes or until golden brown.

❋ Cool for 5 minutes on the cookie sheets. Remove to wire racks to cool completely.

Yield: 20 servings   *Connie McIlwain*

CARAMEL FUDGE SQUARES

2 cups flour
1 teaspoon baking powder
1/8 teaspoon salt
1 (1-pound) package brown sugar
1/2 cup sugar
1 cup cooled melted butter
4 eggs
1 teaspoon vanilla extract

❁ Sift the flour, baking powder and salt together. Combine the brown sugar and sugar in a bowl. Add the butter and mix well. Beat in the eggs 1 at a time. Add the flour mixture and mix well. Stir in the vanilla. Spoon into a buttered 9x12-inch baking pan. Bake at 300 degrees for 45 minutes. Let cool before cutting into squares.

Yield: 24 servings   *Caroline McNeilly*

QUICK BROWNIES

1/2 cup melted butter
1 cup sugar
3/4 cup self-rising flour
5 tablespoons baking cocoa
2 eggs
1 teaspoon vanilla extract
1 cup chopped pecans

❁ Mix the butter, sugar, flour, baking cocoa, eggs and vanilla in a bowl. Stir in the pecans. Spoon into a nonstick 9x13-inch baking pan. Bake at 350 degrees for 20 minutes. Let cool before cutting into squares.

Yield: 24 servings   *Karen Garner*

DOUBLE CHOCOLATE COOKIES

1 (2-layer) package pudding-recipe devil's food cake mix
1/2 cup vegetable oil
2 eggs
1 cup semisweet chocolate chips

❊ Combine the cake mix, oil and eggs in a mixer bowl. Beat at medium speed until blended. Stir in the chocolate chips. Drop by rounded teaspoonfuls 2 inches apart onto a nonstick cookie sheet. Bake at 350 degrees for 10 minutes. Cool on the cookie sheet for 5 minutes. Remove to a wire rack to cool completely.

Yield: 24 servings   *Joann Campbell*

CHOCOLATE PEANUT COOKIES

1 cup butter, softened
3/4 cup sugar
3/4 cup packed light brown sugar
2 eggs
1 teaspoon vanilla extract
1 teaspoon baking soda
1/4 teaspoon salt
2 1/4 cups flour
2 cups chocolate covered peanuts

❊ Mix the butter, sugar, brown sugar, eggs and vanilla in a large bowl. Beat in the baking soda and salt. Add the flour, stirring until a stiff dough forms. Stir in the peanuts. Drop by spoonfuls 2 inches apart onto a nonstick cookie sheet. Bake at 350 degrees for 9 to 11 minutes or until the cookies are lightly browned.

Yield: 48 servings   *Linda Brocato*

Chocolate Peppermint Cookies

2¼ cups flour
1 teaspoon baking powder
¾ teaspoon baking soda
¼ teaspoon salt
¼ cup plus 1 tablespoon baking cocoa
½ cup margarine, softened
½ cup each sugar, packed brown sugar and egg substitute
1 teaspoon vanilla extract
⅔ cup crushed peppermint candy

❀ Mix the first 5 ingredients together. Beat the margarine in a mixer bowl until smooth and creamy. Add the sugar and brown sugar and mix well. Stir in the egg substitute and vanilla. Add the flour mixture gradually, stirring just until blended. Stir in the crushed candy. Drop by level tablespoonfuls onto a cookie sheet sprayed with nonstick cooking spray. Bake at 350 degrees for 10 to 12 minutes or until lightly browned. Cool on a wire rack.

Yield: 44 servings

Amy Darby

Meringues

2 egg whites
⅛ teaspoon each salt and cream of tartar
1 teaspoon vanilla extract
¾ cup sugar
1 cup semisweet chocolate chips

❀ Line a cookie sheet with half a nonrecycled brown paper bag. Beat the egg whites, salt, cream of tartar and vanilla in a mixer bowl until soft peaks form. Add the sugar gradually, beating constantly until stiff peaks form. Fold in the chocolate chips. Drop by rounded teaspoonfuls onto the cookie sheet. Bake at 300 degrees for 25 minutes. Cool on the cookie sheet for several minutes. Lift the cookies gently from the cookie sheet. May add ½ cup chopped pecans.

Yield: 70 servings

Linda Ray

DELICIOUS DATE BARS

1 cup each chopped dates and sugar
3/4 cup water
1 cup packed brown sugar
3/4 cup shortening
1/4 cup butter
2 cups flour
2 1/2 cups rolled oats
1 teaspoon each baking soda and hot water

❀ Bring the dates, sugar and 3/4 cup water to a rolling boil in a saucepan over medium-low heat, stirring occasionally. Boil until thick, stirring frequently. Mix the brown sugar, shortening, butter, flour, oats, baking soda and 1 teaspoon hot water in a bowl. Press half the flour mixture over the bottom of a baking pan. Spoon the date mixture over the flour mixture in the pan. Sprinkle with the remaining flour mixture. Bake at 350 degrees until browned. Cut into bars while hot. Let cool before serving.

Yield: 18 servings   *Melissa Self*

OATMEAL COOKIES

1/2 cup margarine, softened
1/2 cup shortening
1 cup packed brown sugar
3/4 cup sugar
2 eggs
1 teaspoon vanilla extract
1 1/2 cups self-rising flour
3 cups quick-cooking oats

❀ Cream the margarine, shortening, brown sugar and sugar in a mixer bowl until light and fluffy. Add the eggs, vanilla, flour and oats and mix well. Shape into 1-inch balls. Place on a nonstick cookie sheet. Bake at 400 degrees for 8 minutes.

Yield: 24 servings   *Tina Jhin*

Oatmeal Peanut Butter Bars

4 cups (heaping) instant oats
1 cup packed brown sugar
3/4 cup margarine
1 teaspoon vanilla extract
1/4 cup peanut butter
1/4 cup light corn syrup
Peanut Butter Icing

✽ Combine the oats and brown sugar in a large bowl. Mix well and set aside.

✽ Melt the margarine in a saucepan. Add the vanilla, peanut butter and corn syrup and mix well. Add to the brown sugar mixture and mix well.

✽ Press the peanut butter mixture into a 9x13-inch baking pan. Bake at 400 degrees for 15 minutes.

✽ Pour Peanut Butter Icing over the hot crust. Chill until serving time. Cut into bars to serve.

Peanut Butter Icing

1 cup semisweet chocolate chips
1/2 cup butterscotch chips
2/3 cup peanut butter

✽ Combine the chocolate chips, butterscotch chips and peanut butter in a saucepan. Cook until melted, stirring constantly until smooth.

Yield: 48 servings   *Kim Mauldin*

CHEWY PEANUT BUTTER BARS

1/3 cup shortening
1/2 cup peanut butter
1/4 cup packed brown sugar
1 cup sugar
1 teaspoon vanilla extract
2 eggs
1 cup flour
1 teaspoon baking soda
1/4 teaspoon salt
1 1/2 cups grated coconut

❋ Cream the first 4 ingredients in a mixer bowl until light and fluffy. Beat in the vanilla and eggs. Add the flour, baking soda and salt and mix well. Stir in the coconut. Spread in a greased 9x13-inch baking pan. Bake at 350 degrees for 25 minutes or until brown. Let cool before cutting into bars.

Yield: 36 servings   *Jackie Darby*

GOOEY PECAN BARS

1 (2-layer) package butter pecan cake mix
1 egg, lightly beaten
1/2 cup butter
2 eggs
1/2 cup butter
8 ounces cream cheese, softened
1 (1-pound) package confectioners' sugar, sifted
1 1/2 cups chopped pecans

❋ Mix the first 3 ingredients in a bowl. Press over the bottom of a lightly greased 9x13-inch baking pan. Beat the next 4 ingredients in a mixer bowl at medium speed until smooth. Stir in the pecans. Spoon over the cake mix mixture in the pan. Bake at 350 degrees for 45 minutes. Remove from the oven and cover with foil. Bake for 5 to 10 minutes or until set. Let cool before cutting into bars.

Yield: 36 servings   *Simone Mitchell*

Pennsylvania Dutch Cookies

2 cups flour
1/8 teaspoon salt
1 teaspoon cream of tartar
1/2 cup butter, softened
1/2 cup shortening
1 cup sugar
1 egg
1 teaspoon baking soda
1 teaspoon vanilla extract

❁ Mix the flour, salt and cream of tartar together. Cream the butter, shortening, sugar, egg and baking soda in a mixer bowl until light and fluffy. Let stand for 10 minutes. Add the flour mixture gradually, mixing well after each addition. Stir in the vanilla. Drop by teaspoonfuls onto a nonstick cookie sheet. Bake at 350 degrees for 15 to 20 minutes or until the cookies are lightly browned.

Yield: 60 servings   *Jackie Darby*

Scotch-A-Roos

1 cup light corn syrup
1 cup creamy peanut butter
1 cup sugar
6 cups crisp rice cereal
1 cup chocolate chips, melted
1 cup butterscotch chips, melted

❁ Bring the corn syrup, peanut butter and sugar to a rolling boil in a saucepan. Add the cereal and mix well. Press into a buttered 9x13-inch dish. Pour the melted chocolate and butterscotch over the cereal mixture. Let stand until set. Cut into bars. Store in an airtight container.

Yield: 24 servings   *Kaye Mason*

RAISIN LEBKUCHEN

    2³/4 cups flour
    ¹/2 teaspoon baking soda
    ¹/2 teaspoon salt
    1 teaspoon each nutmeg, cinnamon and ground cloves
    ³/4 cup packed brown sugar
    1 egg
    1 cup honey
    1 tablespoon grated lemon peel
    1 teaspoon lemon juice
    1 cup golden raisins
    1 cup toasted blanched slivered almonds
    ¹/2 cup chopped candied citron
    ¹/2 cup chopped candied citron peel
    Lemon Glaze

✿ Sift the flour, baking soda, salt, nutmeg, cinnamon and cloves together and set aside. Cream the brown sugar and egg in a mixer bowl until light and fluffy. Add the honey, lemon peel and lemon juice and mix well. Add the flour mixture gradually, beating at low speed after each addition. Stir in the raisins, almonds, citron and citron peel. Spread the batter in a greased 10x15-inch baking pan. Bake at 375 degrees for 18 to 20 minutes or just until lightly browned; do not overbake. Cool slightly. Brush with Lemon Glaze. Cool completely before cutting into bars. Will keep for up to 1 month in an airtight container.

LEMON GLAZE

    1 cup sifted confectioners' sugar
    1¹/2 to 2 tablespoons lemon juice

✿ Mix the confectioners' sugar with enough of the lemon juice to make of glaze consistency.

Yield: 36 servings   *Lisa Mathews*

White Chocolate Party Mix

5 cups Cheerios
5 cups corn Chex
10 ounces miniature pretzels
2 cups salted peanuts
1½ pounds "M & M's" Chocolate Candies
4 cups vanilla chips
3 tablespoons vegetable oil

❈ Combine the Cheerios, corn Chex, pretzels, peanuts and candy in a large bowl and mix well. Combine the vanilla chips and oil in a microwave-safe bowl. Microwave on Medium-High for 2 minutes, stirring once. Microwave on High for 10 seconds. Stir until smooth. Pour over the cereal mixture and mix well. Spread on waxed paper to cool. Break apart and store in an airtight container.

Yield: 50 servings   *Karran Phillips*

Milk Chocolate Fudge

2 tablespoons margarine
1½ cups sugar
⅔ cup evaporated milk
¼ teaspoon salt
2 cups miniature marshmallows
1½ cups milk chocolate chips
1 cup chopped pecans
1 teaspoon vanilla extract

❈ Bring the margarine, sugar, evaporated milk and salt to a boil in a heavy saucepan over medium heat, stirring constantly. Remove from the heat. Add the marshmallows, chocolate chips, pecans and vanilla, stirring vigorously until the marshmallows are melted. Pour into a buttered 8x8-inch pan. Chill until firm. Cut into squares.

Yield: 18 servings   *Jan Allen*

Ethan and Ashley's Fudge Favorite

1 (1-pound) package confectioners' sugar
1/2 cup baking cocoa
1/4 teaspoon salt
1/4 cup milk
1 tablespoon vanilla extract
1/2 cup butter
1 cup chopped pecans or walnuts

❈ Combine the confectioners' sugar, baking cocoa, salt, milk and vanilla in a large microwave-safe casserole. Mix until partially blended; the mixture will be too stiff to thoroughly incorporate all the dry ingredients. Dot with the butter.

❈ Microwave on High for 2 minutes or until the milk feels warm from the bottom of the casserole. Stir vigorously until the mixture is smooth; any unmelted butter will melt during the stirring. Stir in the pecans. Pour into a waxed-paper-lined dish. Chill for 1 hour in the refrigerator or for 20 to 30 minutes in the freezer. Cut into squares.

❈ To make Peanut Butter Fudge, omit the baking cocoa and add 1/2 cup chunky peanut butter after microwaving.

Yield: 36 servings   *Cindy Ott*

THERE IS AN ALMOST ENDLESS LIST OF MUNDANE CHORES THAT KEEP A LIBRARY VIABLE FOR THE EVERYDAY CARDHOLDER—SHELVING BOOKS, COVERING BOOKS, MENDING BOOKS, CLIPPING NEWSPAPERS, PUTTING UP BULLETIN BOARDS, ENROLLING CHILDREN IN SUMMER READING PROGRAMS. FOR YEARS MSDSL VOLUNTEERS HAVE PERFORMED THESE AND OTHER "TEDIOUS, THANKLESS, NO-GLAMOUR JOBS, AND THEY'VE DONE THEM WITHOUT GRUMBLING," SAYS TERRYE SLEDGE TERRY, VOLUNTEER COORDINATOR FOR THE FLORENCE-LAUDERDALE PUBLIC LIBRARY. HE ADDS, "THANKS, SERVICE LEAGUE, FOR A WHOLE HOST OF JOBS WELL DONE!"

DIVINITY

2 cups sugar
1/3 cup each water and light corn syrup
1/4 teaspoon salt
2 egg whites
1 teaspoon vanilla extract
1/2 cup chopped pecans or walnuts

✳ Combine the sugar, water, corn syrup and salt in a 2-quart microwave-safe casserole. Microwave, covered, on High for 5 minutes; mix well. Microwave, uncovered, on High for 4 to 6 minutes or to 250 to 268 degrees on a candy thermometer, hard-ball stage. Let cool for 3 to 4 minutes. Beat the egg whites in a mixer bowl until very stiff. Pour the sugar mixture in a steady stream over the egg whites, beating constantly until the mixture holds its shape and begins to lose its gloss. Stir in the vanilla and pecans. Drop by teaspoonfuls onto waxed paper.

✳ Note: To avoid any risk of salmonella, heat the egg whites and a small amount of water to 160 degrees on a candy thermometer in a saucepan before using in the recipe.

Yield: 20 servings   *Deirdre Kennedy*

PEANUT CLUSTERS

2 cups each butterscotch chips and semisweet chocolate chips
2 tablespoons peanut butter
1 1/2 cups Spanish peanuts

✳ Combine the butterscotch chips, chocolate chips and peanut butter in a large microwave-safe bowl. Microwave on Medium for 3 minutes; mix well. Microwave on Medium for 2 minutes longer. Stir in the peanuts. Spoon onto a nonstick baking sheet with sides. Chill until firm. Break into pieces.

Yield: 36 servings   *Linda Brocato*

MICROWAVE PEANUT BRITTLE

1 cup sugar
1/2 cup light corn syrup
1 cup roasted peanuts
1 teaspoon butter
1 teaspoon vanilla extract
1 teaspoon baking soda

❈ Mix the sugar and corn syrup in a microwave-safe dish. Microwave for 4 minutes. Stir in the peanuts quickly. Microwave for 4 minutes. Add the butter and vanilla. Microwave for 1½ minutes. Stir in the baking soda. Spoon onto a greased baking sheet with sides. Let cool and break into pieces. May substitute raw peanuts for the roasted peanuts; add with 1/8 teaspoon salt to the sugar mixture before microwaving.

Yield: 10 servings   *Amy Holcomb*

PECAN DELIGHTS

3 cups roasted pecans
2 cups marshmallows
2 cups crisp rice cereal
4 ounces white chocolate, melted

❈ Mix the pecans, marshmallows and cereal in a large bowl. Stir in the white chocolate. Spread by spoonfuls on waxed paper. Let stand until firm.

Yield: 36 servings   *Karran Phillips*

Candied Pecans

    1 teaspoon cold water
    1 egg white
    1 pound large pecan halves
    1 cup sugar
    1 teaspoon cinnamon
    1 teaspoon salt

❀ Beat the cold water and egg white in a small bowl until frothy. Mix with the pecans in a large bowl. Add a mixture of the sugar, cinnamon and salt and mix well. Spread on a baking sheet with sides. Bake at 225 degrees for 1 hour, stirring occasionally.

Yield: 50 servings　　　　　　　　　　　　　　　　　　*Sarah Perry*

Strawberry Candies

    1 (14-ounce) can sweetened condensed milk
    1 pound flaked coconut, finely ground
    1 (3-ounce) package strawberry gelatin
    1 cup finely ground almonds
    1 teaspoon vanilla extract
    1 tablespoon sugar
    1 (3-ounce) package strawberry gelatin
    1 tube green decorator icing

❀ Combine the condensed milk, coconut, 1 package gelatin, almonds, vanilla and sugar in a bowl and mix well. Form by spoonfuls into strawberry shapes. Roll each "strawberry" in 1 package gelatin, coating thoroughly. Let stand until firm. Make the leaves with the green icing. Store in a covered container.

Yield: 40 servings　　　　　　　　　　　　　　　　　*Shawn Nesbitt*

Cakes & Pies

WENDY VAN PELT

WENDY VAN PELT

As an art educator, historian, and consultant, Wendy Van Pelt is recognized for her excellence of painting in various mediums and many styles, ranging from Old Master to abstract and from impressionism to wildlife rendering. Wendy's award-winning art is displayed in corporate collections, galleries, and elegantly appointed homes across North America. Commissions from designers, decorators, and collectors provide the artist with endless challenges and inspiration, as does the rustic setting of her studio off the scenic Natchez Trace Parkway in North Alabama.

GRANNY KELLY'S APPLE CAKE

2 cups each sugar and flour
2 eggs
1 cup vegetable oil
2 cups chopped apples
1 cup chopped walnuts
1/2 cup chopped dates
1/2 teaspoon salt
1 teaspoon baking soda
1 teaspoon apple pie spice
1 teaspoon vanilla extract

❋ Combine the sugar, flour, eggs, oil, apples, walnuts, dates, salt, baking soda, apple pie spice and vanilla in a bowl and mix well; the mixture will be very thick. Press into a 9x13-inch baking pan. Bake at 350 degrees for 45 minutes; do not open the oven door during baking.

Yield: 24 servings   Donna Parkes

PINA COLADA COCONUT CAKE

1 (2-layer) package yellow cake mix
1 (6-ounce) can piña colada mix
1 (14-ounce) can sweetened condensed milk
2 (12-ounce) packages frozen coconut, thawed
2 cups confectioners' sugar
2 cups sour cream
8 ounces whipped topping

❋ Prepare and bake the cake mix using the package directions for a 9x12-inch cake pan. Let cool. Pierce the cake several times with the handle of a wooden spoon. Spoon the piña colada mix over the cake, then the condensed milk. Sprinkle with 1/4 of the coconut. Spread with a mixture of the confectioners' sugar, sour cream and whipped topping. Sprinkle with the remaining coconut.

Yield: 12 servings   Mary Armstrong

BOURBON CAKE

1 (2-ounce) package chopped walnuts
1 (2-layer) package yellow cake mix
1 (4-ounce) package vanilla instant pudding mix
4 eggs
1/2 cup vegetable oil
1/4 cup cold water
3/4 cup bourbon
Bourbon Glaze

❋ Sprinkle the walnuts in a greased and floured 10- or 12-inch bundt pan. Combine the cake mix, pudding mix, eggs, oil, cold water and bourbon in a large bowl and mix well. Spoon into the prepared pan.

❋ Bake at 325 degrees for 1 hour. Cool in the pan for 25 minutes. Invert onto a serving plate. Pierce the cake several times with an ice pick or fork. Pour Bourbon Glaze slowly over the cake, allowing the glaze to soak in.

BOURBON GLAZE

1/2 cup margarine or butter
1 cup sugar
1/4 cup water
1/2 cup bourbon

❋ Combine the margarine, sugar and water in a small saucepan. Boil for 5 minutes. Remove from the heat. Add the bourbon and mix well.

Yield: 16 servings   *Betty Collignon*

CARROT CAKE

2 cups sugar
1 1/2 cups vegetable oil
4 eggs
2 cups flour or cake flour
2 teaspoons baking soda
1 teaspoon salt
2 teaspoons cinnamon
3 cups grated carrots
1/2 cup chopped walnuts or pecans
Cream Cheese Frosting

❈ Combine the sugar and oil in a mixer bowl and mix well. Beat in the eggs 1 at a time. Add the flour, baking soda, salt and cinnamon and mix well. Add the carrots and walnuts and mix well.

❈ Spoon into 3 or 4 greased and floured round cake pans. Bake at 325 to 350 degrees for 45 minutes or until the layers test done.

❈ Spread Cream Cheese Frosting between the layers and over the top and side of the cake.

CREAM CHEESE FROSTING

1 1/2 (1-pound) packages confectioners' sugar
12 ounces cream cheese, softened
1 tablespoon vanilla extract
6 tablespoons butter, softened
1 cup chopped walnuts or pecans

❈ Beat the confectioners' sugar, cream cheese, vanilla and butter in a mixer bowl until smooth and creamy. Stir in the walnuts.

Yield: 12 servings   *Carolyn Wright*

LE DIABLO

> 1 to 2 tablespoons all-purpose flour
> 3/4 cup sugar
> 4 egg yolks
> 6 ounces German's sweet chocolate, chopped or grated
> 3/4 cup unsalted butter
> 1/4 cup cake flour
> 2 tablespoons ground almonds
> 4 egg whites
> 1/8 teaspoon salt
> German Chocolate Frosting

✽ Line an 8-inch round cake pan with waxed paper; spray with nonstick cooking spray. Sprinkle lightly with the all-purpose flour. Beat the sugar and egg yolks in a mixer bowl until creamy. Melt the chocolate and butter in a medium saucepan over low heat. Add the sugar mixture to the chocolate mixture in the saucepan. Cook over low heat until heated through, stirring until blended. Remove from the heat. Mix the cake flour and almonds together. Add to the chocolate mixture and mix well. Beat the egg whites and salt in a mixer bowl until stiff but not dry. Stir 1/4 of the egg whites into the chocolate mixture; fold the chocolate mixture into the egg whites. Spoon into the prepared pan. Bake at 375 degrees for 25 to 30 minutes or until the outside is solid but the center is still creamy. Let cool. Unmold onto a serving plate. Spread German Chocolate Frosting over the top and side of the cake. Serve warm or cold. Garnish with toasted slivered almonds.

GERMAN CHOCOLATE FROSTING

> 3 1/2 ounces German's sweet chocolate, chopped
> 2 to 3 tablespoons coffee
> 3 tablespoons butter

✽ Combine the chocolate, coffee and butter in a saucepan. Cook over low heat until the chocolate and butter are melted, whisking constantly until blended and smooth.

Yield: 8 servings   *Jane Anne Sherrod*

WET CHOCOLATE CAKE

2 cups self-rising flour
2 cups sugar
1/2 cup each margarine and vegetable oil
1 cup water
3 tablespoons baking cocoa
2 eggs
1/2 cup buttermilk
1 teaspoon vanilla extract
1/8 teaspoon salt
1/2 cup margarine
1/3 cup milk
2 tablespoons baking cocoa
1 (1-pound) package confectioners' sugar
1 teaspoon vanilla extract
1 cup chopped pecans or walnuts

❀ Mix the flour and sugar in a mixer bowl. Bring 1/2 cup margarine, oil, water and 3 tablespoons baking cocoa to a boil in a saucepan. Pour over the flour mixture. Add the eggs, buttermilk, 1 teaspoon vanilla and salt and beat well. Spoon into a greased 9x13-inch cake pan. Bake at 350 degrees for 30 minutes. Heat 1/2 cup margarine, milk and 2 tablespoons baking cocoa in a saucepan; do not boil. Pour over the confectioners' sugar in a large bowl. Add 1 teaspoon vanilla and the pecans and mix well. Pour over the hot cake.

Yield: 18 servings   *Linda Brocato*

CHOCOLATE CREAM CAKE

> 1 (2-layer) package devil's food cake mix
> 1/4 cup flour
> 1/2 cup each evaporated milk and water
> 1 cup margarine, softened
> 1 1/2 cups sugar
> 3/4 cup shortening
> 4 teaspoons vanilla extract
> Chocolate Frosting

❊ For the cake, prepare and bake the cake mix using the package directions for two 8-inch cake pans. Cool in the pans for several minutes. Remove to a wire rack to cool completely. Cut each layer into halves horizontally.

❊ For the filling, place the flour in a saucepan. Add the evaporated milk and water gradually, whisking constantly until smooth. Cook over medium heat until thickened, stirring constantly. Let cool. Cream the margarine, sugar and shortening in a mixer bowl until light and fluffy. Add half the vanilla and the flour mixture and beat well. Add the remaining vanilla and beat well. Spread 1/3 of the filling over 1 cake layer. Add 2 more cake layers, spreading each with 1/3 of the filling. Top with the remaining layer. Spread Chocolate Frosting over the top and sides of the cake.

CHOCOLATE FROSTING

> 1/2 cup margarine, softened
> 1 (1-pound) package confectioners' sugar
> 3 tablespoons baking cocoa
> 1/4 to 1/2 cup milk
> 2 teaspoons vanilla extract

❊ Beat the margarine in a mixer bowl. Add the confectioners' sugar, baking cocoa and enough of the milk gradually to make of spreading consistency, beating well after each addition. Beat in the vanilla.

Yield: 12 servings   *Jo Beth Hurt*

AUNT PINY'S POUND CAKE

1 pound butter, softened
2²/₃ cups sugar
8 medium egg yolks
3¹/₂ cups sifted cake flour
¹/₂ cup light cream
8 medium egg whites, beaten
1 teaspoon vanilla extract

✿ Cream the butter in a mixer bowl. Add the sugar gradually, beating constantly until light and fluffy. Add the egg yolks 2 at a time, beating well after each addition. Add the flour and cream alternately, beating well after each addition. Beat in the egg whites at low speed just until mixed. Add the vanilla. Spoon into a lightly greased tube pan. Bake at 300 degrees for 1 hour and 25 minutes. Do not use margarine in this recipe.

Yield: 16 servings   *Kay Adkins*

CHOCOLATE POUND CAKE

3 cups flour
¹/₂ teaspoon each salt and baking powder
¹/₄ cup baking cocoa
1 cup butter, softened
¹/₂ cup shortening
3 cups sugar
5 eggs
1 tablespoon vanilla extract
1 cup milk

✿ Sift the flour, salt, baking powder and baking cocoa into a bowl. Beat the butter and shortening in a mixer bowl until light and fluffy. Add the sugar and eggs and mix well. Stir the vanilla into the flour mixture. Add the flour mixture and milk alternately to the egg mixture, beating well after each addition. Spoon into a nonstick 9- or 10-inch tube pan. Bake at 325 degrees for 1 hour and 20 minutes.

Yield: 16 servings   *Penny Grissom*

Red Velvet Cake

2½ cups sifted flour
1 teaspoon each salt and baking soda
1½ cups sugar
2 cups vegetable oil
2 eggs
¼ cup red food coloring
1 teaspoon vinegar
1 teaspoon baking cocoa
1 teaspoon vanilla extract
1 cup buttermilk
Red Velvet Frosting

❊ Sift the flour, salt and baking soda together and set aside. Cream the sugar and oil in a mixer bowl until light and fluffy. Beat in the eggs 1 at a time. Mix the food coloring, vinegar and baking cocoa in a small bowl. Add to the creamed mixture and mix well. Stir in the vanilla. Add the flour mixture and buttermilk alternately, beating well after each addition.

❊ Spoon into 3 greased and floured round cake pans or one 9x13-inch cake pan. Bake at 350 degrees for 35 minutes or until the layers test done. Cool in the pans for several minutes. Remove to a wire rack to cool completely. Spread Red Velvet Frosting between the layers and over the top and side of the cake.

Red Velvet Frosting

½ cup margarine or butter, softened
1 (1-pound) package confectioners' sugar
8 ounces cream cheese, softened
1 teaspoon vanilla extract
½ to 1 cup chopped pecans

❊ Combine the margarine, confectioners' sugar and cream cheese in a mixer bowl and beat well. Add the vanilla and pecans and mix well.

Yield: 16 servings   *Karen Garner*

German Chocolate Upside-Down Cake

1 cup pecan pieces
1 cup flaked coconut
1 (2-layer) package German chocolate cake mix
1/2 cup melted butter
8 ounces cream cheese, softened
1 (1-pound) package confectioners' sugar

✻ Spread the pecans in a greased 9x13-inch cake pan. Sprinkle with the coconut. Prepare the cake mix using the package directions. Spoon over the coconut. Mix the butter and cream cheese in a bowl. Add the confectioners' sugar gradually, mixing well after each addition. Spoon over the batter. Bake at 350 degrees for 40 minutes. Let cool before cutting into squares.

Yield: 15 servings   Lisa Waldrep

Rum Cake

1 (2-layer) package white or yellow cake mix
1 (6-ounce) package vanilla instant pudding mix
4 eggs
1/2 cup vegetable oil
1/2 cup rum
1/2 cup cold water
1 cup chopped pecans
1/2 cup margarine
3/4 cup sugar
1/4 cup rum
1/4 cup water

✻ Combine the cake mix, pudding mix, eggs, oil, 1/2 cup rum, 1/2 cup cold water and pecans in a mixer bowl and beat well. Spoon into a nonstick 10-inch tube pan. Bake at 325 degrees for 1 hour. Boil the margarine, sugar, 1/4 cup rum and 1/4 cup water in a saucepan for 4 minutes. Pour over the cake in the pan. Let stand for 30 minutes. Invert onto a serving plate.

Yield: 16 servings   Lucy Trousdale

DUTCH APPLE PIE

1 (9-inch) graham cracker pie shell
1 egg white, beaten
5½ cups sliced peeled cooking apples
1 tablespoon lemon juice
½ cup sugar
¼ cup packed brown sugar
3 tablespoons flour
½ teaspoon cinnamon
¼ teaspoon nutmeg
¼ teaspoon salt
¾ cup flour
¼ cup sugar
¼ cup packed brown sugar
⅓ cup butter

❀ Brush the bottom and side of the pie shell with the egg white. Place on a baking sheet. Bake at 375 degrees for 5 minutes or until lightly browned.

❀ Mix the apples, lemon juice, ½ cup sugar, ¼ cup brown sugar, 3 tablespoons flour, cinnamon, nutmeg and salt in a bowl. Spoon into the pie shell.

❀ Mix ¾ cup flour, ¼ cup sugar and ¼ cup brown sugar in a bowl. Cut in the butter until crumbly. Sprinkle over the apple mixture. Bake for 50 minutes or until the filling is bubbly and the topping is golden brown.

Yield: 8 servings   *Leigh Ann Morrison*

Blueberry Pie

1 cup sour cream
2 tablespoons flour
3/4 cup sugar
1 teaspoon vanilla extract
1/4 teaspoon salt
1 egg, beaten
2 1/2 cups drained rinsed fresh blueberries
1 unbaked (9-inch) pie shell
3 tablespoons flour
3 tablespoons unsalted butter, softened
3 tablespoons chopped pecans or walnuts

❖ Blend the sour cream, 2 tablespoons flour, sugar, vanilla, salt and egg in a bowl. Fold in the blueberries. Spoon into the pie shell. Bake at 400 degrees for 25 minutes. Sprinkle with a mixture of 3 tablespoons flour, butter and pecans. Bake for 10 minutes. Let stand until cool. Chill until serving time.

Yield: 8 servings — *Penny Joiner*

Buttermilk Pies

4 eggs
2 cups sugar
1/2 teaspoon salt
2 tablespoons flour
1/2 cup melted butter
1 teaspoon vanilla extract
2/3 cup buttermilk
2 unbaked (8-inch) pie shells

❖ Beat the eggs in a bowl. Add the sugar, salt, flour, butter and vanilla and mix well. Stir in the buttermilk. Spoon into the pie shells. Bake at 325 to 350 degrees until the center is set.

Yield: 16 servings — *Carolyn Wright*

CHOCOLATE PIE

1¹/₄ cups sugar
¹/₂ cup flour
3 tablespoons baking cocoa
2 cups water
3 egg yolks
¹/₄ cup margarine or butter
¹/₈ teaspoon salt
1 teaspoon vanilla extract
1 baked (9-inch) pie shell
3 egg whites
6 tablespoons sugar
3 tablespoons water

✲ Mix 1¹/₄ cups sugar, flour and baking cocoa in a large saucepan. Add enough of the 2 cups water to make a paste. Beat in the egg yolks. Heat the remainder of the 2 cups water, margarine and salt in a small saucepan until the margarine is melted, stirring frequently. Add to the flour mixture and mix well. Cook until thickened, stirring frequently. Remove from the heat and stir in the vanilla. Spoon into the pie shell.

✲ Combine the egg whites, 6 tablespoons sugar and 3 tablespoons water in a double boiler. Cook over low heat until the mixture registers 160 degrees on a candy thermometer, beating constantly with a hand mixer. Remove from the heat. Beat at high speed until stiff peaks form. Spread over the pie filling. Bake at 400 degrees until the meringue is lightly browned.

Yield: 8 servings   *Kathy Brewer*

Quick Key Lime Pie

8 ounces whipped topping
1 (14-ounce) can sweetened condensed milk
Juice of 2 Key limes
Grated peel of 1 Key lime
1 (9-inch) graham cracker pie shell

❈ Combine the whipped topping, condensed milk, lime juice and lime peel in a bowl and mix well. Spoon into the pie shell. Chill until set or overnight. Garnish with lime slices.

Yield: 8 servings   *Betty Collignon*

Strawberry Pie

1 cup sugar
2 tablespoons cornstarch
1 cup water
¼ cup strawberry gelatin
1 quart strawberries, hulled, sliced
1 baked (9-inch) pie shell
8 ounces whipped topping

❈ Bring the sugar, cornstarch and water to a boil in a saucepan. Cook until the mixture is clear, stirring frequently. Stir in the gelatin. Let cool. Reserve some of the strawberries for a topping. Fold the remaining strawberries into the gelatin mixture. Spoon into the pie shell. Top with whipped topping. Top with the reserved strawberries.

Yield: 8 servings   *Betty Collignon*

NUTRITIONAL PROFILE GUIDELINES

The editors have attempted to present these family recipes in a form that allows approximate nutritional values to be computed. Persons with dietary or health problems or whose diets require close monitoring should not rely solely on the nutritional information provided. They should consult their physicians or a registered dietitian for specific information.

ABBREVIATIONS FOR NUTRITIONAL PROFILE

Cal — Calories   T Fat — Total Fat   Sod — Sodium
Prot — Protein   Chol — Cholesterol   g — grams
Carbo — Carbohydrates   Fiber — Dietary Fiber   mg — milligrams

Nutritional information is computed from information derived from many sources, including materials supplied by the United States Department of Agriculture, computer databanks, and journals in which the information is assumed to be in the public domain. However, many specialty items, new products, and processed foods may not be available from these sources or may vary from the average values used in these profiles. More information on new and/or specific products may be obtained by reading the nutrient labels. Unless specified, the nutritional profile of these recipes is based on all measurements being level.

❋ Artificial sweeteners vary in use and strength so should be used "to taste," using the recipe ingredients as a guideline. Sweeteners using aspartame (NutraSweet and Equal) should not be used as a sweetener in recipes involving prolonged heating, which reduces the sweet taste. For further information on the use of these sweeteners, refer to the package.

❋ Alcoholic ingredients have been analyzed for the basic ingredients, although cooking causes the evaporation of alcohol, thus decreasing caloric content.

❋ Buttermilk, sour cream, and yogurt are commercial types.

❋ Cake mixes that are prepared using package directions include 3 eggs and 1/2 cup oil.

❋ Chicken, cooked for boning and chopping, has been roasted.

❋ Cottage cheese is cream-style with 4.2% creaming mixture. Dry curd cottage cheese has no creaming mixture.

❋ Eggs are all large. To avoid raw eggs that may carry salmonella, as in eggnog or 6-week muffin batter, use an equivalent amount of commercial egg substitute.

❋ Flour is unsifted all-purpose flour.

❋ Garnishes, serving suggestions, optional information, and variations are not included.

❋ Margarine and butter are regular, not whipped or presoftened.

❋ Milk is whole milk, 3.5% butterfat. Low-fat milk is 1% butterfat. Evaporated milk is whole milk with 60% of the water removed.

❋ Oil is any type of vegetable cooking oil. Shortening is hydrogenated vegetable shortening.

❋ Salt and other ingredients to taste as noted in the ingredients are not included in the profile.

❋ If a choice of ingredients is given, the profile reflects the first option. If a choice of amounts is given, the profile reflects the greater amount.

Pg. No.	Recipe Title (Approx Per Serving)	Cal	Prot (g)	Carbo (g)	T Fat (g)	% Cal from Fat	Chol (mg)	Fiber (g)	Sod (mg)
11	Artichoke Dip	98	1	4	9	83	8	1	231
11	Hot Artichoke Dip	71	2	1	7	88	8	<1	107
12	Artichoke Black-Eyed Pea Dip	172	5	10	12	63	19	2	507
12	Hot Bacon and Swiss Dip	249	7	3	23	84	48	<1	268
13	Fabulous Broccoli Dip	76	3	3	6	74	9	1	243
13	California Dip*	59	1	2	5	79	4	<1	124
14	Cheese and Onion Dip	517	15	3	49	86	121	<1	562
14	Chili Cheese Dip	75	4	2	5	66	18	<1	197
15	Incredible Cheese Dip	55	3	<1	5	75	14	<1	233
15	Feta Cheese and Walnut Dip	203	7	5	18	78	22	1	284
16	Mexican Cheese Log	55	1	1	5	86	17	<1	58
16	Paige's Cheese Spread	73	3	1	6	80	18	<1	141
16	Easy Fruit Dip	29	<1	3	2	49	5	0	17
17	Olive Spread	44	<1	<1	5	94	8	<1	120
17	Green Olive Tapenade	41	<1	<1	5	95	0	<1	191
18	Pico de Gallo	17	<1	2	1	51	0	<1	2
18	Quick Dip	69	3	1	6	76	19	<1	110
19	Homemade Salsa	6	<1	1	<1	2	0	<1	154
19	Seafood Cocktail Spread	50	2	3	3	58	11	<1	138
19	Shrimp Dip	60	3	<1	5	78	28	<1	56
20	Steamed Shrimp Dip	92	7	1	7	67	63	<1	250
20	Salmon Mousse	78	3	1	7	81	23	<1	166
21	Monterey Jack Salsa	189	5	5	17	78	17	2	452
21	Sombrero Dip	129	10	6	7	50	32	1	666
22	Hot Spinach Dip	101	4	3	9	74	25	1	280
23	Taco Dip	52	4	3	3	52	12	1	156
23	Tomato Cheese Spread	307	8	5	30	84	41	1	442
24	Vegetable Spread	85	<1	1	9	94	8	<1	122
25	Heart of a Choke	168	7	21	7	37	5	6	397
25	Artichoke Crostini	97	3	8	6	57	7	1	181
26	Cheese Straws	129	4	8	9	61	13	<1	127
26	Rice Krispies Cheese Straws	51	1	3	4	64	10	<1	86
27	Cheese Strips*	78	2	5	5	65	7	<1	99
27	Marinated Cheese	117	3	2	11	81	20	1	135
28	Tuscan Grilled Chicken Bites*	315	18	8	24	68	44	3	682
29	Fig and Apricot Torte	249	6	24	15	51	25	1	75
29	Ham Roll-Ups	90	2	1	9	85	16	<1	114
30	Stuffed Mushrooms	143	8	5	11	65	31	1	297
30	Easy Shrimp-Stuffed Mushrooms	880	26	6	84	85	160	1	1169
31	Toasted Pecans	246	2	5	26	88	17	2	63
31	Cold Pizza	Nutritional information for this recipe is not available.							
32	Quesadillas	406	17	17	31	67	81	1	493
33	Sausage and Cheese Muffins	57	2	5	3	50	5	<1	116
33	Easy Hot Sausage with Sorghum	271	5	38	11	36	27	0	358
34	Sausage Mushroom Pâté	319	9	14	26	71	102	1	592
35	Pickled Shrimp	285	18	3	23	72	161	<1	1445
36	Shrimp Pizza	92	3	5	7	64	22	<1	160
36	Taco Roll-Ups	189	7	13	12	58	33	1	431
37	Tortilla Pinwheels	103	2	7	7	64	28	1	190
38	Tapenade with Crostini	44	2	7	1	19	1	<1	161

Pg. No.	Recipe Title (Approx Per Serving)	Cal	Prot (g)	Carbo (g)	T Fat (g)	% Cal from Fat	Chol (mg)	Fiber (g)	Sod (mg)
39	Coffee Cooler	76	2	9	3	38	5	0	51
39	Mocha Blend	63	<1	12	1	19	0	<1	1
40	Coffee Kahlúa Punch	93	1	11	4	34	13	0	42
40	Fruit Punch	39	<1	10	<1	1	0	0	6
41	Hot Percolator Punch	95	<1	24	<1	1	0	<1	4
41	Pleasing Punch	76	<1	19	<1	0	0	<1	7
42	Hot Buttered Rum	355	1	65	4	10	15	1	38
42	Summer Tea	56	<1	15	<1	0	0	<1	4
45	Sharon's Pumpkin Bread	281	3	41	12	37	35	1	187
46	Diana's Crawfish Bread	499	21	62	20	35	55	4	1051
47	Banana Nut Bread	288	4	42	12	37	56	2	219
47	Baby Butterball Biscuits	100	1	7	8	70	20	<1	172
48	Blue Pete's Sweet Potato Biscuits	270	5	44	8	27	21	2	458
49	Cheese Biscuits	45	1	3	3	66	3	<1	47
49	Easy Corn Bread	397	6	30	29	64	88	3	530
50	Beer Rolls	77	1	11	3	39	10	<1	19
50	Monkey Bread	630	7	72	36	52	47	3	1288
51	Cinnamon Rolls	356	4	55	14	34	24	1	95
51	Raisin Bran Muffins	118	2	20	4	27	12	1	173
52	Apple Raisin Bran Muffins	194	4	37	4	19	18	2	209
53	Blueberry Muffins	73	1	13	2	26	6	<1	8
54	Baked Apple Doughnuts	244	2	34	11	41	18	1	255
54	Pancakes	388	11	41	20	47	148	1	843
55	Sour Cream Coffee Cake	283	3	34	15	48	64	<1	276
56	Glazed Sour Cream Walnut Coffee Cake	659	9	85	33	44	122	2	533
57	Breakfast Roll	509	18	34	33	59	115	0	509
57	Breakfast Pizza	340	17	13	24	64	156	<1	738
58	Egg Puffs	260	16	5	19	67	173	<1	673
58	Cheese and Egg Fondue	528	31	22	35	59	304	1	735
59	Sausage Mushroom Breakfast Casserole	217	11	6	16	68	92	<1	652
59	Gourmet Grits	330	11	17	24	66	92	<1	574
60	Fresh Tomato Tart	173	5	12	12	61	24	<1	258
63	Artichoke Soup	154	7	18	8	42	7	8	937
63	Broccoli Soup	282	16	19	16	52	54	2	918
64	Brazilian Black Bean Soup	238	12	43	3	10	0	9	735
65	Cheese Soup	341	15	23	21	55	66	2	977
65	Potato Soup	381	7	17	32	75	46	1	732
66	Baked Potato Soup	441	15	29	30	60	55	2	602
67	Gazpacho	134	3	18	7	44	0	3	595
68	Tomato Basil Soup	80	2	8	5	53	12	2	226
69	Easy Ground Beef Vegetable Soup	419	30	29	21	44	90	5	877
70	Mexican Taco Soup	207	14	23	7	29	28	5	796
70	Chili	423	35	17	24	51	112	6	826
71	Brunswick Stew	302	30	30	7	20	51	5	1441
72	Classic Lamb Stew	361	33	27	8	24	91	4	795
73	Cherry Congealed Salad	256	3	32	14	47	23	1	71
73	Holiday Cranberry Mold	191	2	37	5	22	0	2	1
74	Mandarin Orange Salad*	502	7	30	41	71	0	5	28
75	Strawberry Pretzel Salad	733	7	88	39	48	78	2	674
75	Baked Fruit Salad	298	2	54	10	29	21	3	152

Pg. No.	Recipe Title (Approx Per Serving)	Cal	Prot (g)	Carbo (g)	T Fat (g)	% Cal from Fat	Chol (mg)	Fiber (g)	Sod (mg)
76	Frozen Banana and Pineapple Salad	276	3	43	12	37	36	2	90
76	Frozen Fruit Salad	603	4	55	43	62	92	5	248
77	Fruit Salad	117	1	17	6	40	0	2	6
77	Fruit Cocktail Salad	216	1	55	<1	1	0	2	185
78	Artichoke Rice Salad	288	4	16	24	73	14	3	664
78	Congealed Asparagus Salad	243	2	19	18	66	13	1	302
79	Black and White Bean Salad	125	7	23	1	5	0	6	523
79	Fresh Corn and Black-Eyed Pea Salad	224	6	30	11	42	0	3	190
80	Colorful Cabbage Salad*	295	1	26	22	65	0	2	252
81	Corn Salad*	109	2	13	6	48	7	2	604
82	Mom's German Potato Salad**	234	4	21	15	58	68	2	195
82	Dijon and Dill Potato Salad	150	2	18	8	46	7	1	568
83	Salad with Feta Cheese Dressing*	174	3	6	16	81	8	1	413
84	Mixed Greens with Sweet Hot Dressing*	313	3	27	23	63	0	2	19
85	Green Salad with Strawberries and Honey Dressing*	924	8	67	73	69	33	3	580
86	Crunchy Romaine Tossed Salad*	558	5	38	45	70	16	3	276
87	Layered Spinach Salad	210	7	16	13	56	23	2	272
87	Spring Salad	114	1	7	10	73	0	2	175
88	Cherry Tomato Salad	166	2	10	14	72	0	3	320
88	English Pea Congealed Salad	247	3	15	20	72	18	2	310
89	Greek Pasta Salad with Balsamic Vinaigrette*	291	8	40	11	34	11	3	198
90	Primavera Salad*	343	16	31	18	46	20	3	986
91	Terrific Tortellini Salad	388	16	43	16	38	52	2	727
91	Fruity Chicken Salad	598	21	29	45	67	83	4	509
92	Chicken Salad with Orange Vinaigrette*	487	17	21	38	70	64	2	406
93	Curried Chicken and Orange Salad	416	42	9	23	50	122	1	400
94	West Indies Salad*	195	13	3	15	68	57	1	173
94	Honey Poppy Seed Dressing	93	<1	6	8	76	7	<1	62
97	Meatballs	578	37	55	24	37	179	1	1079
97	Barbecued Meatballs	406	28	29	19	43	87	1	1379
98	Meat Loaf	373	28	20	19	47	132	2	592
98	Beef Stroganoff	762	57	44	39	46	191	1	980
99	Fireside Fillets in Mushroom Sauce*	1030	42	8	91	80	209	1	985
100	Rouladen	366	44	4	18	46	120	1	376
101	Roast Tenderloin of Pork with Mustard Sauce	559	42	6	39	64	191	<1	324
102	Fletcher's Pork Chops	335	25	3	24	63	101	<1	654
102	Impossible Bacon Pie	505	26	27	32	58	275	<1	747
103	Creole Black Beans	574	27	70	21	33	44	2	1812
104	Oven-Baked Jambalaya	257	14	24	11	41	113	1	680
105	Basil Grilled Chicken	631	54	<1	45	65	251	<1	620
106	Chicken Breasts Parisian Style	545	61	9	29	48	221	3	853
107	Citrus Grilled Chicken*	399	54	7	16	37	154	<1	336
107	Lemon Mustard Chicken	355	54	2	13	35	146	<1	584
108	Raspberry Chicken	401	54	3	18	40	182	1	179
109	Chicken in Sour Cream	585	25	53	29	45	70	1	871
109	Susie's Chicken and White Sauce	554	53	1	35	59	173	<1	1490
110	Chicken Quesadillas	982	71	89	37	34	178	6	1612
111	Hot Chicken Salad Pie	774	17	22	68	80	85	2	1047
111	Roasted Duck Breast	824	34	4	74	81	235	1	1326
112	Comeback Sauce	71	<1	2	7	90	4	<1	95

Pg. No.	Recipe Title (Approx Per Serving)	Cal	Prot (g)	Carbo (g)	T Fat (g)	% Cal from Fat	Chol (mg)	Fiber (g)	Sod (mg)
112	Great White Barbecue Sauce	62	<1	1	7	95	6	<1	743
115	Coquilles St. Jacques Baumanière	684	25	36	45	60	268	1	1044
116	Shrimp Creole	312	15	45	8	23	90	3	2855
117	Marinated Shrimp Kabobs*	494	29	74	9	16	202	5	1113
118	Skillet Barbecued Shrimp	839	45	3	71	76	590	<1	2159
119	Shrimp Scampi	279	15	5	21	67	135	<1	408
119	Crab Meat and Vegetable Pie	197	13	18	7	34	143	2	364
120	Seafood, Chicken and Artichoke Casserole	509	50	32	20	34	164	6	700
121	Grilled Tuna Steaks	635	27	7	55	78	42	0	5936
121	Tartar Sauce	54	<1	2	5	88	4	<1	125
122	Beefy Tomato-Stuffed Shells	380	18	31	22	50	40	5	629
123	Lasagna	501	35	27	28	51	147	3	1226
124	Veal Piccata over Angel Hair Pasta	1057	64	77	51	44	220	3	1216
125	Marinated Chicken Breasts in Pepper Fettuccini*	695	33	29	49	63	171	2	533
126	Chicken Pecan Fettuccini	642	28	34	46	62	156	4	721
127	Chicken Pasta*	480	29	47	15	29	73	4	990
128	Chicken Capellini	504	25	31	31	56	77	4	666
129	Fettuccini Alfredo	541	17	34	39	63	115	2	739
129	Pasta with Broccoli and Mushrooms	851	27	78	49	50	51	8	1978
130	Penne Pasta with Tomatoes, Olives and Two Cheeses	593	25	61	29	43	53	5	1179
133	Stuffed Artichokes	287	13	34	12	37	10	8	777
133	Basic Asparagus Casserole	204	9	7	16	69	84	1	499
134	Baked Beans	354	19	51	10	24	48	6	852
134	French Bean Bundles	Nutritional information for this recipe is not available.							
135	Broccoli Casserole	322	9	16	25	71	82	3	1032
135	New Year's Day Sauerkraut	152	2	6	9	54	23	4	1154
136	Sweet-and-Sour Carrots	196	2	36	6	29	0	3	434
136	Corn Slaw	279	4	32	15	49	16	3	463
137	Fresh Corn Loaf	197	9	24	8	35	70	3	899
137	Baked Corn with Sour Cream	220	6	26	12	45	16	2	427
138	Eggplant Parmesan	243	10	31	11	37	12	2	1427
138	Mushroom Casserole	407	14	20	31	67	89	1	681
139	Vidalia Deep-Dish	367	7	29	25	61	53	2	234
139	Hopping John	160	13	20	3	15	23	3	866
140	Twice-Baked Potatoes	352	10	35	19	49	61	3	367
140	Cheesy Potato Casserole	288	12	20	18	56	46	1	714
141	Marinated Potato Slices	365	3	28	27	67	0	2	246
141	Scalloped Potatoes	159	8	21	5	27	14	2	376
142	Celery and Garlic Mashed Potatoes	365	4	22	30	72	96	2	195
142	Spinach Cheese Bake	386	8	22	30	71	117	3	758
143	Spanakopita	568	21	43	35	55	66	5	1392
144	Country Club Squash	313	9	13	26	73	62	3	553
145	Zucchini Toss	54	3	6	3	42	1	2	102
145	Vegetables and Dill	56	2	8	3	36	0	3	352
146	Vegetable Casserole	229	5	21	15	56	18	3	910
146	Macaroni Casserole	577	19	27	43	68	82	1	810
147	Consommé Rice Casserole	225	4	22	13	53	<1	1	569
147	Dirty Rice	309	27	18	14	41	78	2	449
148	Yorkshire Pudding	141	6	20	4	25	76	1	242
148	Brown's Relish	112	1	28	<1	2	0	1	6

Pg. No.	Recipe Title (Approx Per Serving)	Cal	Prot (g)	Carbo (g)	T Fat (g)	% Cal from Fat	Chol (mg)	Fiber (g)	Sod (mg)
151	Bu's Apple Dumplings	317	3	52	12	33	17	2	433
152	Banana Split Cake	436	3	54	23	47	53	2	200
152	Bananas Foster	329	3	44	15	40	50	2	135
153	Mini Blintzes	58	1	11	3	37	12	<1	64
154	Cherry Chiffon Dessert	307	4	55	8	23	13	1	58
154	Chess Squares	288	3	43	12	36	45	<1	259
155	Mother's Chocolate Fluff	591	7	65	34	52	53	2	581
156	Cream Cheese Pastry	277	4	27	17	55	48	<1	322
157	Fruit Pizza	Nutritional information for this recipe is not available.							
158	Peach Cobbler	632	6	99	25	35	70	2	272
158	Nutty Peach Crisp	833	7	99	48	51	89	4	800
159	Punch Bowl Cake	296	3	46	11	34	30	1	243
160	Snow on the Mountain	301	3	36	15	47	3	1	128
161	Martha's Blueberry Pecan Cheesecake	453	4	43	28	57	21	2	271
162	Chocolate Cheesecake	383	10	41	20	47	85	1	284
162	Chocolate Chip Cheesecake	561	6	53	34	56	44	2	199
163	"M & M" Cheesecake Squares	229	3	22	15	57	30	1	109
164	Spring Breeze Cheesecake	429	4	37	29	61	44	<1	270
164	Apple Pudding	290	2	52	9	27	23	2	163
165	Lemon Soufflé with Raspberry Sauce	319	5	38	17	47	161	<1	55
166	White Chocolate Crème Brûlée	708	7	40	58	73	381	0	79
167	Lemon Velvet Ice Cream	367	6	59	13	30	92	1	84
167	Lime Sorbet	59	<1	15	<1	0	0	<1	<1
168	Grandmother's Peach Ice Cream	327	5	44	15	42	56	1	67
168	Homemade Vanilla Ice Cream	506	8	47	32	56	214	0	159
169	White Chocolate and Macadamia Nut Cookies	236	2	22	16	60	29	1	60
170	Caramel Fudge Squares	205	2	31	9	37	56	<1	129
170	Quick Brownies	122	2	13	8	55	28	1	94
171	Double Chocolate Cookies	171	2	22	9	46	18	<1	181
171	Chocolate Peanut Cookies	116	2	14	6	47	20	<1	84
172	Chocolate Peppermint Cookies	74	1	13	2	24	<1	<1	73
172	Meringues	20	<1	4	1	30	0	<1	6
173	Delicious Date Bars	308	3	48	12	34	7	2	102
173	Oatmeal Cookies	199	3	28	9	39	18	1	145
174	Oatmeal Peanut Butter Bars	125	3	15	7	48	<1	1	57
175	Chewy Peanut Butter Bars	101	2	11	6	50	12	1	73
175	Gooey Pecan Bars	215	2	25	12	51	38	<1	169
176	Pennsylvania Dutch Cookies	58	1	7	3	52	8	<1	43
176	Scotch-A-Roos	229	4	36	10	36	<1	1	145
177	Raisin Lebkuchen	149	2	31	2	13	6	1	64
178	White Chocolate Party Mix	251	3	31	12	44	2	1	92
178	Milk Chocolate Fudge	212	2	39	9	39	3	0	57
179	Ethan and Ashley's Fudge Favorite	99	1	14	5	44	7	1	43
180	Divinity	114	1	25	2	15	0	<1	41
180	Peanut Clusters	134	2	13	9	56	<1	1	15
181	Microwave Peanut Brittle	210	4	35	7	30	1	1	151
181	Pecan Delights	94	1	7	8	69	1	1	20
182	Candied Pecans	76	1	6	6	68	0	1	48
182	Strawberry Candies	Nutritional information for this recipe is not available.							
185	Granny Kelly's Apple Cake	237	2	30	13	47	18	1	107

Pg. No.	Recipe Title (Approx Per Serving)	Cal	Prot (g)	Carbo (g)	T Fat (g)	% Cal from Fat	Chol (mg)	Fiber (g)	Sod (mg)
185	Piña Colada Coconut Cake	826	9	109	41	44	65	3	511
186	Bourbon Cake	407	4	45	19	42	54	1	376
187	Carrot Cake	952	9	112	54	50	118	2	580
188	Le Diablo	486	7	45	34	60	165	2	114
189	Wet Chocolate Cake	429	3	60	21	42	24	1	307
190	Chocolate Cream Cake	844	6	99	48	51	58	1	586
191	Aunt Piny's Pound Cake	463	5	50	28	53	164	<1	265
191	Chocolate Pound Cake	428	5	57	20	42	100	1	233
192	Red Velvet Cake***	649	5	63	43	59	43	1	346
193	German Chocolate Upside-Down Cake	509	4	62	28	49	77	1	456
193	Rum Cake	412	4	46	22	47	53	1	442
194	Dutch Apple Pie	439	3	74	15	31	21	2	334
195	Blueberry Pie	324	3	38	18	49	51	2	201
195	Buttermilk Pies	246	3	33	12	42	69	<1	249
196	Chocolate Pie	346	4	56	12	32	80	1	217
197	Quick Key Lime Pie	398	5	54	17	39	17	1	234
197	Strawberry Pie	302	1	48	11	33	0	2	107

* Nutritional Profile includes entire amount of marinade, dressing, and/or sauce.
** Nutritional Profile does not include 1/4 cup pickle juice.
*** Nutritional Profile does not include 1/4 cup food coloring.

Index

The Art of Cooking

Muscle Shoals District Service League
P.O. Box 793
Sheffield, Alabama 35660
205-389-9191

Please send me _____ copies of *The Art of Cooking* ... $19.95 each _____

Alabama residents add state sales tax . . . . 1.60 each _____

Postage and handling . . . . 4.50 each _____

Total Enclosed _____

Method of Payment: ❑ Check ❑ Visa ❑ MasterCard

Card Number _____ Expiration Date _____

Name _____

Address _____

City _____ State _____ Zip _____

Make checks payable to The Art of Cooking

Photocopies are accepted.